Miracles

*"For this cause
the people also met him
for that they heard
that he had done
this miracle."*
(John 12:18 KJV)

Miracles

Stories edited and compiled
by Joanie Hileman

Miracles
(Formerly titled *This Miracle and Maine Miracles*)

Copyright 2008, Amlin Publishing.

This book may be copied and freely distributed.
Its contents belong to God; its work for his glory.

Printed in the United States of America
through Lightning Source.

Amlin Publishing Paperback edition / May 2008

Amlin Publishing Paperbacks are published by Amlin
Publishing Inc. through Lightning Source,
a subsidiary of Ingram Industries Inc.,
Nashville, TN

Contents

I Am Here, Mary's Story	8
Good Things, Bryon and Ruthie's Story	11
The Door, Lisa's Story	14
All Things, David's Story	19
Judgment Day, Ken and Jeanette's Story	36
Distance, Ruthie's Story	43
The Hiding Place, Herb and Flo's Story	45
The Sobering Truth, Bob's Story	48
Stuck, Cathy's Story	58
Little Warrior, Eryn's Story	59
Jolted, Dave's Story	88
Katahdin, Jamie's Story	89
Our Daily Bread, Laura's Story	92
The Cross, Larry's Story	94
Erika's Angels, Julie's Story	97
Pierced, Nancy's Story	104
Make It Blue, Stephanie's Story	114
Take My Hand, Sandy's Story	115
That Still Small Voice, Jean's Story	120
The Nurse's Aide, Marie's Story	121
A Simple Prayer, Autumn's Story	126
Take My Life, Jeremiah's Story	128
From Dealer to Healer, Chuck's Story	136
The Appointment, Kim's Story	149
Salt and Light, Elizabeth's Story	153
Heaven, Lily's Story	159
Tracy's Song, Joanie's Story	161
My Shield, Daniel's Story	165
Losing Matthew, Barbara's Story	167
Heaven Bound, Belinda's Story	183
The Gift, Joan's Story	195
Taylor, Betsy's Story	198

Foreword: *Me?* Write a Book?

I'm not trained as a writer, and I never finish long projects, so when I felt the Lord was leading me to write a book of miracles, I was doubtful. But he was persistent, and I was convinced.

Here's how it happened:

In 2001, at a Calvary Chapel service, my pastor mentioned miracles. He was teaching from the book of Luke when he started chasing a rabbit and found himself up in a tree with a coworker.* The coworker said, "I've never heard of any miracles happening around here." But my pastor told this man, "I've heard of hundreds of miracles."

But that's where he left it! Instead of telling us about miracles, he suddenly jumped out of the tree and started walking back towards the subject, leaving me on the edge of my seat. Miracles in Bangor, Maine? I wanted to hear about them!

So when the book, *My God Story,* by Bobby Coy from Calvary Chapel, Fort Lauderdale, came out, I bought it and read it. *Twenty-six people. Twenty-six stories. One God.* It's a book of miracles, and it's very good.

For months the book sat on my shelf, but then one day I took it down to loan to a friend. Before giving it to her, I scanned some of the stories. After giving it to her, I started having this thought: *I should write a book like that.*

Over and over, for days and days, the thought haunted me. *I should write a book like that.*

So finally, I prayed, "*God?* Are *You* putting this thought into my head, or is this just me looking for a way to get attention?

I should write a book like that. (There it is again.)

"Lord, I know I'm a decent writer, and I think writing is fun and all—but if you want me to write a *whole book...*"

I should write a book like that.

The thought wouldn't leave me alone, BUT I didn't want to say anything, because if I told people about it—then I might actually have to *DO* something.

Finally the thought tortured me enough that I just had to tell someone! And when I told my friend Nancy, her enthusiasm surprised me. "My heart just filled with JOY when you said that! What an *awesome* idea! What an *amazing* way to tell people about the Lord!"

So I interviewed Nancy, who just happened to have a story to share, but it took *months* to write up the rough draft, and I did a terrible job. Clearly I was imagining things. God hadn't called me to write a book.

I should write a book like that--still the thought wouldn't leave me alone.

Then, a different kind of thought. *Who am I kidding? It's obvious I don't have time for this. What will I have to sacrifice to get it done? My kids? My house? I'll waste years of my life, and no one will publish it anyway. Forget it. It's a TOTAL waste of time!*

So I pretty much gave up on the idea, until one day when I was reading a *Focus on the Family* magazine. A scripture jumped right off the page, smacked me in the head, and jumped directly into my heart. "... be ye steadfast, unmovable, always abounding in the work of the Lord, forasmuch as ye know that your labor is *not in vain* in the Lord." (1 Corinthians 15:58, emphasis added)

So I finished a story, but it took a *long* time. Then another thought started haunting me. *Look how long it took to write one little story. I can't write a whole book! This is stupid. This is a GIANT, huge, big honkin' thing, and I never finish long projects! Remember the quilt? And that cross stitch thing that's been in the drawer for fifteen years? I'LL FAIL. I'll never get it done.*

Then, right on cue, our pastor taught us a new song. "The GIANT's calling out my name, and he laughs at me, reminding me of all the times I've tried before and failed. The giant keeps on telling me, time and time again, (girl) you'll never win. You'll *never* win. But the voice of truth tells me a different story." *(I should write a book like that.)* "The voice of truth says do not be afraid." *(Your labor is not in vain in the Lord.)* "The voice of truth says this is for My glory. Out of all the voices calling out to me, I will *choose* to listen and believe the voice of TRUTH."**

"Alright already!" I prayed. "I'll stop listening to the voices of doubt, and I'll listen to your voice only, Lord. I WILL write that book—juuust as soon as I get caught up with my housework."

So every night, at around 9:30, I gathered up the few brain cells that were still awake, and together we'd sit in front of the computer—not doing much of anything.

Then one Sunday morning during worship at church, the Lord spoke loud and clear to my spirit. In an almost audible voice, I heard, *"You need to sacrifice your house."* A moment later Matthew 6:33 came to mind. "But seek first his kingdom and his righteousness, and all these things will be given to you as well." I took this to mean that I needed to put the book first, and that somehow my other work would get done.

So after that, every morning I'd get my kids off to school, spend some time in the Word, then I'd walk past the kids' nightclothes on the floor, the breakfast dishes, the laundry, the toys (and all of the other STUFF that never goes away no matter how much you work at it) and I'd sit down at my computer, where I (and all of my rested little brain cells) worked together to edit miracle stories! Then later when my brain was completely fried, I'd do housework. (Did you know it only takes two brain cells to fold laundry, and one and a half to vacuum?)

So even though I might have to live in a less than perfect house (BIG giant understatement) and it might take me twelve months to get the Christmas decorations down, I have finally found amazing satisfaction and peace in fully submitting to the will of God!

It took two years to get through to me, 'cause I'm not the smartest knife in the drawer, but eventually I realized, God can use *anyone* to do *anything*, if only we are willing to take his hand and go where he leads. And right now, if you are holding a finished copy of *Miracles* in your hands, it's all God's work—because I'm not trained as a writer, and I never finish long projects.

J. H.

> ***"being confident of this,***
> ***that he who began a good work in you***
> ***will carry it on to completion..."***
> (Philippians 1:6 NIV)

---

*Pastor Ken is somewhat notorious for chasing rabbits (and then *miraculously* finding his way back to the subject unscathed.) When Calvary Chapel Bangor was brand new, Ken paid the bills by working in tree removal.

**Voice of Truth by Casting Crowns

The following stories fall into five basic categories;

angel stories,
salvation,
healing,
God's provision,
and God's protection.

Some contain elements of more than one of these categories. The large majority occurred in or near central Maine. In only a couple have the names been changed for confidentiality purposes. While a few may not be as *miraculous* as the rest, they are still touching stories of how God's people have been moved to show His love in amazing ways. To the best of this writer's knowledge, based on the moral character of the people who shared their stories, as well as documents, etc., the stories are true.

And one more thing, finding these miracles was not difficult. Although miracles can happen to anyone at anytime, as far as this writer can tell, they are relatively common among those who have chosen to surrender their lives to the Lord Jesus Christ.

A big hug to Nancy
for her unparalleled enthusiasm.
A warm thanks to all of the precious people
who shared their miracles.
And my heart, my soul, my all, to my God,
who hasn't given up on me yet.

I Am Here
Mary's Story

The sky was overcast, and the smell of rain was in the air when we got the call.
Union Street. Car accident. A bad one.
We bolted for the ambulance. It was 9:30 p.m.
Noise. Noise at the scene. *So loud.* Sirens *blared.*
Traffic backed up. Rescue workers shouted to be heard above the **NOISE.**
Even still, I could hear her.
A two year old. Lying in the street.
Screaming. Screaming. **SCREAMING!**
A woman knelt by her. Holding her head.
Gently. Firmly.
Don't move, Dear One. Don't be afraid. I am here.
I ran to her side. **"Keep her still! Can you keep holding her?! I need more equipment!"**
The woman nodded. So calm. So very calm.
I got the equipment. We secured her.
And it was time to move.
Still the woman helped. We carried her, ever so slowly, *so slowly,* the few yards to the ambulance—one, inch, at a time.
"Don't let her move her head!"
Be calm, Little One, Precious Child. I am here.
The girl had quieted a bit by the time we got her into the ambulance.
I set to work quickly, stabilizing her, securing her. Quickly.
It was pouring rain now.
The woman stood outside the ambulance.

In the pouring rain.
Watching. Listening.
As I secured the child the woman spoke up.
"Would it be alright if I left now?"
She stood in the rain.
Yes. I told her yes.
She could go. I was all set. Thank you!
Back to my work. Several seconds passed, and I looked up. I needed to get her name.
She deserved more. She deserved a reward!
I looked out the back of the ambulance.
I looked out the windows.
The lights were bright, they lit up the whole area.
I should have been able to see her walking away.
But she was gone.

Two doctors in Bangor, and one in Boston,
all said the same thing.
"Why is this little girl alive? She should have died."
Her neck was broken.
She should have died.
But she didn't.
Someone was holding her.
Holding her still.
Still. Be still, Little One.
I am here.

> *Mary believes this woman was a guardian angel—and it's not the first time she has had this thought.*

Jesus said,
***"Take heed that
ye despise not one of these little ones;
for I say unto you, That in heaven their angels
do always behold the face of my Father..."***
(Matthew 18:10 KJV)

Angels, ministering spirits, continually riveted on the face of the Father, waiting on the edge of their seats, for the next command to head for the ladder.

***"...and behold a ladder
set up on the earth, and the top
of it reached to heaven: and behold
the angels of God ascending
and descending on it."***
(Genesis 28:12 KJV)

Good Things
Bryon and Ruthie's Story

Relocating to a new state, with seven children, during a recession, wasn't the easiest thing in the world to do, but time and time again, God was faithful to provide.

One Christmas I found myself unemployed, and Ruthie and I found ourselves at the Good Will store trying to buy gifts for seven kids—with twenty dollars. As you can imagine, it was hard finding anything in the piles of *junk* that had already been picked over. But somehow we managed to find seven junky little toys, so our kids would at least have *something* to open on Christmas morning.

Feeling depressed and desperate, we took the long way home and started looking for money along the side of the road. I remembered a story my grandfather had told me about a time when he was desperate for money. His car had broken down, and he'd found a hundred dollars on the side of the road. So, as we rolled slowly along, we scanned the roadside and saw something that looked like money blowing in the wind. But when we got out, we found it was only a piece of paper, and when we got back in, we were more depressed than ever.

We didn't think it was right to pray for gifts, because we know Christmas is about Jesus. (Besides, there were more important things we needed to be praying about: we hadn't paid the mortgage, we barely had enough money to buy food, and everyone needed clothes...) But our hearts were broken, and we desperately wanted our kids to be blessed on Christmas, so sitting there in the car, we cried and apologized, but then we asked the Lord to *please* bless our kids.

> ***"And whatever we ask,
> we receive from Him, because
> we keep His commandments and do
> those things that are pleasing in His sight.
> And this is His commandment, that
> we should believe on the name
> of His Son Jesus Christ..."***
> (1 John 3:22-23 MKJV)

On Christmas Eve the crappy little toys were wrapped and sitting underneath the pathetic looking Charlie Brown tree we had found in the field. And Ruthie and I were feeling about as horrible as we could possibly feel. But then the phone rang. It was a couple we had met once or twice, relatives of some church friends. We barely knew them, but they wanted to know if they could come over.

They arrived in a fifteen passenger van, and came to the door asking if the kids could help them carry in a couple of things. A *couple* of things! It turned out, the van's rear seats had been removed, and the whole vehicle was packed to the roof with packages! The kids brought in load after load, until the little tree was completely buried and gifts were spilling out into the room. Then they started hauling in groceries!

We didn't have enough money to buy a Christmas turkey, but they brought everything, boxes and boxes of food, enough for a huge Christmas dinner, and enough to last for awhile after that.

We will never forget what our six year old daughter, Callie, said as she stood in front of the open refrigerator. "Look, Mom! We're rich with milk!" To this day we still say this. We know if we can afford to buy milk, we're rich!

The next morning when the gifts were opened, we didn't find cheap plastic toys from the grocery store. We found high quality, brand new toys like thirty dollar Tonka trucks. There were also practical gifts such as winter coats and boots. Someone had taken the time to find out the kids' ages and sizes, likes and needs. Everyone got exactly what they needed!

There were hundreds, if not thousands, of dollars worth of gifts and food given to us that night. And to this day we still don't know where it all came from. But as we stood there watching load upon load of good things being brought into our house, we felt as if the Lord was saying, "*This* is my heart toward you. I *want* to bless you." It *is* the Lord's heart to bless his children.

And this experience taught us something: Our best is nothing but *junk* compared to what the Lord can do!

> **"If you then, being evil, know how to give good gifts to your children, how much more shall your Father in heaven give good things to those who ask him!"**
> (Matthew 7:11 MKJV)

The Door
Lisa's Story

On the outside I looked the same, but on the inside
I had changed so much, I didn't even know
who I was anymore.

We kept seeing this ad on TV. This guy, an athlete, kept telling us how much his life had changed, and he said if we ordered this book, it would change our lives too. So my husband ordered it. But then we just put it on the shelf and never gave it another thought.

That is, until I found myself out of work (again) and I just *happened* to come across this book. I had plenty of time on my hands, with nothing better to do, so I started reading it. I don't remember the name of the book, but it had quotes from the Bible and stories about how God had changed people's lives, and the one thing it kept coming back to, time and time again, was how there was this "door" and that this "door" was Jesus.

Jesus said, "I am the door:
by me if any man enter in, he shall be saved,
and shall go in and out, and find pasture."
(John 10:9 KJV)

As I read I began to think about my life. It was a total mess. My anger had caused me to lose yet another job; every night I headed over to my neighbor's to get drunk; there were days when I was so depressed all I wanted to do was drive off the road into a tree; and to top it all off, my marriage was failing. So as I read, I thought about how my life was a complete disaster—and I started wondering about this "door."

At the end of the last chapter, there was a prayer, so I said it. I got down on my knees, and I asked Jesus to come into my heart and save me.

But I didn't feel any different.

So I got up and went on with my day. But the thing about the *door* would not leave my mind, and it was still with me as I walked down to the end of the driveway to get my mail. When I opened the mailbox, it was empty, except for one small postcard advertisement that said, **"The Doors Have Been Opened."** Two big golden gate doors were pictured, and at the bottom it said, "Front Row Video."

I stared at this postcard all the way back up to the house, but then I heard the phone ringing. It was a friend of mine. She wanted to tell me about a job opening at a local restaurant, and by the time I hung up the phone, the *door* was forgotten. I drove down to the restaurant and put in an application, and the next day I was interviewed and got the job.

Then slowly things began to change. I still headed to my friend's every night, but I couldn't drink as much anymore; it made me feel sick. So my drinking slowly decreased, and I didn't miss it. Then when my friend moved away, I stopped altogether.

My marriage was ending, and I was planning on quitting my job, but one of my coworkers encouraged me to stay. The very next day, I was asked if I wanted to work in the bakery, and it was there that I met Shaun. We became instant friends, and almost immediately he started telling me about how God had changed his life.

As time went on, my attitude became completely

different. I was rarely angry anymore and I almost never got depressed. I stopped blaming everyone else for my problems and I stopped being so focused on what *I* wanted. More and more I started to really *see* people, and appreciate them for who they were. Then I began attending a little church down the street from my house, and it was here that my daughter asked Jesus into her heart. Soon after this, my sister and I, and our two daughters, were baptized.

Gradually Shaun and I became closer and then started dating. During this whole time, I kept thinking about how *lucky* I had become; everything seemed to be going so well for me. But I just chalked it all up to coincidence—until something happened that made me stop and think.

Just before Shaun and I were to be married, we were looking for a house. We needed something halfway between Thorndike, where Shaun was going to be working, and my daughter's house in Eddington. So we prayed about it. We asked God to help us find a nice place halfway between Thorndike and Eddington.

Every day Shaun took the interstate to work, but on this particular day, he decided to take it slow and drive up Route 9 instead. As he passed through Hampden, he saw a *For Rent* sign in the window of a house and called the number immediately. The man who answered the phone was amazed; he had just put the sign up that very minute!

Later that day we went and looked at the house. It was *perfect;* a nice house in Hampden, and all the man wanted for rent was four hundred dollars. He didn't want any deposit, and he said we didn't need to pay the rent right away if we didn't have it. It seemed too good to be true, but it *was* true, so we gladly told the man we'd take it.

Later that week I measured the miles from

Thorndike to Hampden to Eddington. The driveway of the house in Hampden was *exactly* (to the tenth of a mile) halfway between Shaun's work and my daughter's house!

So I began to wonder if the things happening were more than just luck.

Then one day I found myself in front of a mirror. On the outside, I looked the same, but on the inside I had changed so much, I didn't even know who I was anymore. And as I stood there looking at my reflection, I suddenly remembered the day, the one where I had gotten down on my knees and prayed for Jesus to come into my heart. *That* was the day when everything had begun to change! I had opened the door, and miracles had begun to happen.

> ***"Therefore if any man be in Christ, he is a new creature: old things are passed away; behold, all things are become new."***
> (2 Corinthians 5:17 KJV)

When you ask God for something, and it happens, don't think it was just luck. No matter what it is, thank God for it because he actually did do it. Come to the realization that he really does exist and that he really does care. Don't look for big giant miracles to take place. Don't wait for lightning to strike. Just thank him for the small things. And when you finally acknowledge him and say "Thank you, God," that's when he smiles and says, "No problem. I'll do it again."

The day I prayed that prayer, something *real* happened, even though I didn't feel it. Jesus says if you open the door, he will come in, and he means it. The day I prayed that prayer, Jesus stepped through the open door of my heart and quietly began to work on me.

***Jesus said, "Behold,
I stand at the door and knock:
if any man hear my voice, and open
the door, I will come in..."***
(Revelation 3:20 KJV)

It's that simple.

All Things
David's Story

"I may have to go with your God theory—
because this cannot be explained medically."

David: Dear Lord, I would like to see a miracle here on earth. I know that you can perform miracles—but I just want to see one with my own eyes.

The phone call:
"Hello."
"Mrs. Chrisos. —Is David there?"
"Gosh no. David's at school."
"No. No. He never showed up. —Some kids who just came up Broadway said there was a car just like David's. They're pretty sure it was David's car. He—he was in a pretty bad car accident... Mrs. Chrisos?"

A moment later:
"Yeah."
"Don it's Terri! Where are you?"
"I'm right in town, heading out Broadway. Why? What's wrong?"
"I just heard David was in a bad accident out past Kev-Lan. You should be there."
"What? What happened?"
"I don't know, I just heard it was bad."
"Alright. Okay. I'm almost there now."

When I arrived at the scene of the accident, the ambulance was already gone, and I was thankful for the few minutes warning I'd gotten from Terri because if I had seen my son's car unprepared, I think I would have lost it. It was teetering sideways on a four foot bank of ice on the opposite side of the road. The passenger side was flattened, and the rear tire was sticking out sideways. The bumper was hanging by one bolt and folded into a V, and where the rear window had been, a jumbled mess of interior jutted out. I pulled open the driver's side door and peered in. All but a small space around the driver's seat had been completely mangled.

David?

The five minute drive to St. Joseph Hospital felt like an hour. This can't be happening. This can't be happening. I can't believe this! Please let him still be alive. Oh, God please don't let him die!...

When David's father arrived at the hospital, pastors from his church and several other people were already there praying. The seventeen year old was in critical condition, with blood, and bandages, and tubes coming out everywhere. But at least he was alive, and there was still time to pray.

As soon as the news reached Bangor Christian School, high school classes were canceled, and people started praying.

After being moved to Eastern Maine Medical Center, David was given a CT scan. The results revealed a massive brain injury. David was given drugs to keep him in a coma in an effort to minimize further swelling in his brain. The next three days would be critical.

Every moment at least one family member stayed by David's side. If it wasn't Mom or Dad, it was brother Jonathan, or Billy. Twenty-four hours passed, and the neurologist became concerned. By this time the swelling should have subsided, David should have been responding more. A second CT scan was ordered. David's brain was still swelling.

For three days, David remained in a drug induced coma. For three days, David breathed with the help of a respirator. And for three days, people continued to pray.

Finally the doctors decided it was safe to take David off the drugs, and the family waited anxiously for him to wake up. But he didn't.

Another day went by, and, on Sunday afternoon, a nurse came in to talk with the family. "The waiting area is packed with people wanting to see David," she said. "We took the chairs out to make more room, but they just keep coming. Do you want to come out and see them before we start sending them away? We just finished counting; there are 144 people out there."

Only two of the 144 were relatives. The rest were friends and people whose lives had been touched by David in one way or another. Throughout the day, people continued to pack the waiting area. Since it was tournament time, entire basketball teams showed up to offer words of encouragement. One man who had traveled all the way from Calais summed up the general feeling. He told the family, "I'm not really surprised that David would draw this many people. It isn't because he's a great athlete, which he is, it's because he's a great kid."

A Great Athlete:

To say this high school junior was a great athlete was something of an understatement. As a captain for the Bangor Christian Schools' baseball team, David had been awarded the title Most Valuable Player two years in a row. As a captain for the golf team, he was MVP three times and had taken second in the State his junior year. As a captain for the basketball team, he was chosen MVP twice, was a member of the Penobscot Valley All Star Team, and had been selected as one of Maine's Best Basketball Tournament Players.

From the time he'd started kindergarten, David had been telling people that he and his friends were going to win the States in basketball for their small Christian school. And it had looked like that goal would be realized. As a starting guard his junior year, David had led the team in minutes played and scored an average of sixteen points per game. The Patriots had just finished a 17-2 regular season, and were in the number one seeding heading into the Eastern Maine Basketball Tournaments.

A Great Kid:

Not only did David excel in sports, but he was on the National Honor Roll, was the Junior Class Treasurer, the National Honor Society Vice President, and a student tutor. He was a volunteer for the Children's Miracle Network, The Salvation Army, United Way, the local soup kitchen, missions projects, and vacation bible school. And on top of everything else, he still found time to coach Pee Wee basketball and soccer.

For David, serving others was something that came naturally. David's mom reports: "From the time he was a little boy David was always willing to help in any way he could. Whether he was doing household chores, visiting an elderly neighbor, or giving money to a homeless person, his sensitivity towards others was always apparent."

She goes on to say, "David told us about a boy at school who always ate lunch by himself on the front steps because some kids had ostracized him for his weight. At least once a week, David made it a point to sit outside with this boy. Some weeks he sat with him several days, and after awhile other kids started joining them. One day towards the end of the year, David told me there were ten kids out there! So we knew David had a lot of friends, but the large numbers of people visiting the hospital made us realize that he had touched more lives than we had ever imagined."

In the early hours of Monday morning, four days after the accident, David regained consciousness. Later that day, an MRI was taken. The results were devastating. David had sustained a "near fatal" brain injury. His frontal lobe, his rear lobe, and multiple areas in between were injured. The family was prepared to expect the worst. He would need to relearn many things, his personality might be completely changed, and he might never be able to live independently. —So people continued to pray.

"He's awake! He's awake!"

David's father ran back into the hospital room where he saw his son's eyes wide open—for the first time in four and a half days. The boy had an awful headache, but when his basketball coach entered the room, David immediately asked about their quarterfinal game. When he learned it was only a few hours away, he said, "I'll be up and running soon. I don't think I can start, but I'll give you a few minutes off the bench." This brought tears to his father's eyes because here was the David he had always known. He knew at that moment that they were going to have to chain this boy down, so he would have time to heal.

When the nurse began to ask David questions about his age, where he went to school, where he lived, the positions he played in sports, etc. David was able to answer *every* question! The nurse was *blown* away. She couldn't understand how someone with such extensive brain injury was answering questions as though nothing had happened. But when she asked about the accident, he remembered nothing, except one thing he would later tell his parents.

"When my car got hit, God reached out his hand, and I grabbed it."

When the Patriot's basketball team entered the Bangor Auditorium later that morning, David's number 34 was painted on faces, written on sneakers, and scrawled across banners throughout the stadium. Perhaps the biggest cheer of the game was heard during the introductions, when David's name was announced. David's teammates knew, beyond a shadow of a doubt, that he would want them to go on without him, because David did *not* like to lose. At all. The news of his waking inspired the Patriots to run faster, jump higher, and play with the most devastating press Bangor Christian fans had seen all season. The result was unrelenting pressure that caused fifteen unanswered points in the first quarter, forced twenty-one turnovers in the first half, and brought the team to a 79-54 victory. They were doing it for David, and they were NOT going to let him down!

David was happy when he heard about the game, but he was still fading in and out of consciousness, and he still didn't understand what had happened to him.

"Mom, why am I here?"
"You had an accident."
"I did?"
"Yes."
"What happened?"
"You hit black ice."
"Oh. —Did I kill anyone?"

"No."
"Was Greg in the car?"
"No. He didn't need a ride."
"Oh. —So I was the only one who got hurt?"
"Yes."
"—Mom?"
"Yes?"
"Am I in the hospital?"
"Yes, David, you're in the hospital."
"What happened?"
"You were in an accident."
"Was anyone killed?"

This went on for several days, but gradually David began to put the pieces together. "So I was in an accident. I hit black ice. Greg wasn't in the car. No one was killed..."

When David was told he would need to go through extensive physical, occupational, and speech therapy, a Bible verse entered into his mind, and he assured his parents that he was going to be just fine. In the days, weeks, and months to come, whenever he was faced with a new challenge, he gave his best effort and rested in the promise, "I can do all things through Christ who strengthens me." (Philippians 4:13)

The first time David got up to take a shower, the nurse told the family they would need to explain everything to him step by step. She said to show him the soap and to explain what it was for, etc., but when David got into the shower, he knew exactly what to do. He didn't need any help at all.

"I can do all things through Christ who strengthens me."

> ***"...pray one for another,***
> ***that you may be healed..."***
> (James 5:16 MKJV)

Eight days after the accident, a conference was called. The rehab doctor looked at the MRI, appeared baffled, and said, "With such extensive injury to the brain, your son should not be doing what he is doing at such an early stage of recovery. I cannot explain this."

David's father piped up. "I can explain it," he said. "So many people have been praying for our son, and the Lord is answering our prayers."

The doctor didn't know what to think. He had been a rehabilitation doctor for over thirty years and he had never seen anything like this. Finally he said, "I may have to go with your God theory—because this cannot be explained medically."

When more scans were taken, only a few injured areas remained.

The family was told it would take David an entire year to complete physical therapy. He finished in three and a half *weeks*. He made more progress in that time than most people with his kind of brain injury make in two *years*.

The family was told it would take two years for David to complete speech therapy. David finished in six months. At the end of the six months, the therapist said, with tears in her eyes, "When he can do better than I can, it's time to say goodbye." David had blessed her so much, she hated to see their time together come to an end.

In the spring David went back to school for half days. With the help of a tutor, he worked into the summer and was able to complete his junior year—with high honors.

The following was written by David's brother Jonathan, and first appeared in the Bangor Christian School Patriot's newsletter a few months after David's accident:

It's amazing how a single event, a brief moment in time, an unexpected incident can change a person's life forever. It's amazing how God allows events to happen, how He helps us to understand that everything happens for a reason, and how He gives us amazing strength and peace to get through it.

It was February 14, my first class was at 9:30, and I had plans like every other Valentine's Day to wallow in self-pity for not having "A Big Day of Love Fest" planned. At 7:58, while I was getting ready to go to class, a car, headed to 1476 Broadway, hit a patch of black ice, and spun out of control into oncoming traffic. The high impact collision left a BCS teenager unconscious and barely breathing.

This would not be my typical Valentine's Day. To my chagrin, my wallowing was about to get a lot worse. Boycotting the patron saint's Valentine's Day and bemoaning an A- I received on a recent exam were about to move down the list in my directory of "The World's Greatest Problems."

After we received the call – the call everyone hopes they never get – my mom and I bolted for the door and were off to Broadway. I was praying for a fender bender, hoping for the best, not expecting the worst. When my dad called on the cell phone and told me, "It's bad. Go to St. Joe's," I knew I needed to get prepared for the worst.

When we arrived at St. Joseph's, our pastors and some friends were already there, waiting for us to arrive. I don't know how exactly to describe the mood. Maybe "calm panic" would work. Except for my mom, her mood is easy to describe: panic heart-brokenness. Definitely nothing calm about it. The St. Joseph's people told us to go to the family room. There they would talk to us. At this point everyone who had gathered at the hospital began crying and my mom passed out. I suppose you mothers would understand.

In the family room, basically we found out they were doing some tests, and we really wouldn't know anything for a while. Oh, and it was a while! All we could do was wait and pray and pray and pray. Did I mention we were praying a lot?

Finally, I asked a nun if I could go in and see my brother. That was a big mistake. I thought I wanted to see him, but in the condition that he was in, I should have stayed in the family room. I walked into his room in the emergency ward. He was just lying there. Tubes coming out from everywhere you can put a tube, head bleeding and bandaged, his clothes were in shreds on the floor. I grabbed his arm, and although he was unconscious, we prayed together. It is a scene that will be etched in my memory forever.

After a couple of hours, he was transferred to EMMC where he would stay for three weeks. The first week he spent in the ICU, five days of it in a coma. For three weeks we continued to get news from the medical community that was not as positive as we would have liked. But what they did not realize, when they were quoting us statistics, is that we have an all-powerful Father in heaven on our side ... a Father who would be cheering for David every step along the road to recovery ... a Father who has been with David his whole life and was in the car the morning of February 14. I remember David telling my dad in the hospital, "When my car got hit, God reached out his hand, and I grabbed it."

David has never been bitter, never asked "why," and he has had an amazing testimony for the Lord. In fact, he thanks the Lord every day for saving his life and that the accident happened to him and not to one of his friends or family members.

It hasn't been easy for him either. He works so incredibly hard every day to be even better than he was before his accident. I am proud to call him my brother. He inspires me every day and challenges me to look at the world differently.

While he was in the hospital, I had a lot of time to think. I thought too much actually. But I often wondered, unlike David, why this had to happen to him. I would think, "He's a good kid, and he didn't deserve this." I know many other people thought this as well. A very wise woman in my church gave me a remarkable answer. "When God was looking for someone for this to happen to, He knew David could handle it and would be a good witness and example for Him. It's an honor."

WOW! I wasn't expecting that. I asked her if she thought David would be okay. Another good answer, "No matter the outcome, remember that God is always good. Sometimes He is gracious. I am praying that He will be gracious." WOW again. God *is* good, and He has also been gracious.

Now that David is home and doing so well, I have been doing some more thinking. Oh no, here we go. Why did our family, friends, church community, even strangers drive, fly, and travel from all over the state and country to be with us? Why did they sit for hours in the hospital waiting room when they knew there was nothing they could do? Why did we receive countless cards, meals, balloons, and flowers? Why are people still praying for David?

People are good and people are loving. No – people are incredible. From our entire family, thank you, everyone!

Although I didn't realize it at the time, Valentine's Day 2002 taught me that love is more than a dozen over-priced roses, a cupid-shot arrow through the heart, an expensive meal, or a Britney Spear's valentine that says, "I hope your Valentine's Day is a big hit!" Love is people pulling together and praying, visiting, and crying for hours at a time with a family who is going through a rough time. Love is God sending an angel to be with someone when they need it most. Love is cards, meals, and flowers from a sincere heart. I learned more about love. I learned to appreciate life and enjoy every moment of it. I learned that sometimes it takes a tragedy to bring people to their knees in prayer. Although I didn't realize it at the time, "A Big Day of Love Fest" *was* planned – people from all over showed their love to the Chrisos family.

"I'm sure you hear it all the time,

but how's Dave doing?" It's a question I never mind answering because it gives me a chance to talk about three really cool things: the love of God, my "miracle boy" little brother with the awesome attitude, and the goodness of people. David always wanted to see a miracle on earth. Not only did he see one, he is one. David shouldn't have been able to go back to school this year; he shouldn't have been able to be on the high honor roll; he shouldn't be able to ace tasks in therapy, and he shouldn't be able to play basketball this summer. But he has done all these things, and he will be playing this summer! Go number 34 ... Maine loves you, and we are proud of you! Thank you, God, for being good ... and gracious. It's amazing how a single event, a brief moment in time, and an unexpected incident can change a person's life forever.
—Jonathan Chrisos

The following year, instead of trudging his way through physical therapy, David was back to playing golf, basketball, and baseball, and was All State in all three sports. In his first basketball game since the accident, David scored thirteen points, including the game-winning basket. For the rest of the season he averaged fourteen points per game, and before the season was over he reached the 1,000 point mark for his high school basketball career.

During his final year in high school, David was a

student tutor, a teacher's assistant, a coach for Pee-Wee basketball, Treasurer for the Fellowship of Christian Athletes, Vice President for the National Honor Society, and was voted Who's Who among America's high school students. He also volunteered with the Booster Club, the local soup kitchen, vacation bible school, Praise Puppets ministry, The Children's Miracle Network, The New York City Missions Project, and the Baseball Dugout Project.

"I can do all things through Christ who strengthens me."

Out of approximately 14,000 student athletes, who were nominated for the 2002 Wendy's High School Heisman Award, two seniors from Bangor Christian Schools were chosen as state finalists. David was one of them. They were asked to write an essay about one of their heroes. David wrote about his father. The other BCS finalist wrote about David. From the New England states as well as New York, a winner was chosen to represent the northeast region. David was that winner.

By the end of his senior year, only sixteen months after his accident, David received over $200,000 in scholarship offers, and he was accepted at every college he applied to including the prestigious Wheaton College, which has been called "the Harvard of Christian colleges." He received a full academic scholarship to Eastern Nazarene College in Massachusetts, where he decided to attend, and went on to play three years of college basketball as one of the team's top players. He has kept up a grade point average of 3.5 or higher and continues to touch the lives of others through volunteer opportunities.

Recently David proposed marriage to his girlfriend of two years, and she said, "Yes."

Because of his accident, David's lifelong dream of

winning the high school basketball state championship was never realized, but he was never bitter. In fact he is thankful for the accident and will gladly tell anyone who will listen, "My recovery was a miracle, the very miracle I asked the Lord to allow me to witness. He is the reason I am here today, and I hope to touch people's lives by telling them what God has done for me. Some people think my healing was luck, but I tell them no. People prayed for me, and God did a miracle. And if my story is bringing people closer to the Lord, then I would gladly go through it all over again."

Just this last semester, as a senior in college, David earned a grade point average of 4.0. And David says,

> ***"I can do all things through Christ who strengthens me."***
> (Philippians 4:13 MKJV)

> ***"...With men this is impossible; but with God all things are possible."***
> (Matthew 19:26 KJV)

David's car.

David helping mom with the vacuuming.

Judgment Day
Ken and Jeanette's Story

Ken: Life is full of injustices and unfair deals, but if people will just stop and invite the God of the universe into their lives, justice will be served. Sometimes it's on the other side of suffering, but justice *will* be served.

Jeanette: Once again, it was time to put Micah on the plane to go visit his father. Once again, I worried about his care and safety. And once again, I cried. He was my baby, only nine years old, and he had to travel from Maine to California, all by himself, to spend the entire summer with the man who had abused me for years.

Tom had never abused our son, but, because of his lifestyle and involvement with drugs, I worried constantly. At best, Tom would be a bad influence. At worst, well, I would try not think about the worst.

So Ken and I hugged our boy one last time, prayed again that the Lord would watch over him—then watched as he boarded the plane.

> *Tom vowed to make Jeanette's life miserable if she ever left him and threatened revenge if she took Micah away. But after nine years of abuse, despite the threats, she decided to leave. She filed for divorce, and the court awarded her full custody of Micah.*
>
> *And Tom stayed true to his word; he stalked her, he threatened her over phone, and he took her to court five times trying to*

win custody of his son. Even after she married a pastor and moved to Maine, he still found ways to harass her.

The day after we put Micah on the plane, we received a phone call from our lawyer in California. Micah had been *severely* beaten. Tom had taken several photographs showing cuts and bruises all over his body. Our lawyer had seen them; he said they were real—and Tom was accusing *Ken* of child abuse!

I was *panicked*. Micah was fine when we put him on the plane. Something *horrible* had happened! But *what?* Was he assaulted on the plane? Was there some kind of accident? Did *Tom* do this?

Ken: I wanted to kill him. He was behind this, there was no doubt. He was always making threats, detailed threats about burning people with acid or breaking their bones... One time he hired a thug to beat up a teacher who had given him a bad grade. So I figured he would do something dirty like this. And I wanted to kill him!

Jeanette: Was Micah okay? Would Ken be convicted of child abuse? Would I lose custody of my son?! What would happen with the church? And what about Jessica, our new baby? Would DHS try to take *her* away?!

We called our Maine lawyer immediately. All he could say was, "I don't know what's going on here, but pray hard and get to California."

So we prayed. I fell on my face before the Lord and begged him to get us out of this. The next day we called everyone we knew and asked them to pray. We had people over to the house for prayer, and I even called the 700 Club. They were having a telethon, and when I called, they prayed for us right there on the show. So people all over the nation heard about us and were praying.

Then Ken called Tom.

Ken: I still wanted to hurt him. I was torn up constantly, *frustrated,* and enraged that anyone would accuse me of abusing a child! Especially this particular child. I loved Micah. But I had to *choose* to put my anger aside. I had to choose to leave things with the Lord; *He* would take care of things. So I called Tom, and told him what the scriptures have to say about what he had done.

> ***"He who digs a pit shall fall into it,***
> ***and he who rolls a stone shall***
> ***have it turn back on him."***
> (Proverbs 26:27 LITV)

> ***"The wicked have laid a snare for me;..."***
> (Psalm 119:110 KJV)

> ***"...but the wicked shall fall by his***
> ***own wickedness."***
> (Proverbs 11:5 KJV)

Jeanette: Getting on that plane to face charges of child abuse was probably the hardest thing I have ever done. Here I was, I had everything, and in a matter of minutes it could all be gone. The evidence against us was strong—and our lawyers said there was nothing we could do.

So we prayed for a miracle.

When we arrived at my mother's house in California, she told us our lawyer had called and wanted us to go to his office right away. There was new evidence against Tom! We were allowed to witness the evidence, but were told to say *nothing* about it. What had been a civil case was now a *criminal* case, and if Tom found out about it, he would be sure to skip town, and if that happened, we would probably never see him—or Micah again.

The next day at the courthouse, when the elevator doors opened, there was Tom and his lawyer. I thought Ken was going to kill him.

Ken: I wanted to kill him—just get in, close the doors, and *KILL him.* The lawyer took one look at me and started frantically pushing buttons to get the doors closed. Then they didn't want me in the courtroom at all. But finally when someone asked me if I would ever hurt a woman, I said, "No!" So they decided to let me go in with a female secretary on each arm.

Jeanette: First the judge announced that new evidence had been brought forward, then Tom's lawyer stood up and said he was resigning from the case. Tom stared at him with a look that said, *"What?"*

A woman came through the doors, walked up the aisle, and handed the judge a tape. Tom was *panicked!* He stood up and said, "Your Honor, I resign, I don't want to press charges, I don't..."

But the judge told him to, "*Sit* down!" He put the tape in the player, looked at Tom—and pressed play.

A woman's voice could be heard. "That's how you made those bruises was with grease pencils?"

The judge bent the microphone down to the speaker.

"Yes, we used grease pencils." (That was Tom's voice.)

"I thought you said you used putty?"

"Yes, putty and grease pencils. To get the creases in the broken skin, we used putty..."

> ***"The wicked are trapped***
> ***by their own words..."***
> (Proverbs 12:13 GNB)

> ***"(God) will turn their own tongues***
> ***against them and bring them to ruin;"***
> (Psalm 64:8 NIV)

Ken: It was like a vision of Judgment Day! I was siting off to the left and a little behind Tom, and as the tape played, his bald head just got redder and redder. He started protesting, but the more he protested, the more you could identify the voice on the tape! He bragged about how he had drugged Micah and hired a makeup artist to paint cuts and bruises on his body, he boasted about beating *me* up, and then he started mocking the judge, saying, 'The (blankety-blank) judge bought the whole thing hook line and sinker!'"

Jeanette: At this point the judge pressed pause and looked at Tom. He pressed rewind, then stop, then played it again, all the time glaring at Tom with a look that said, *"You* have *had it!"*

Tom stood up and said, "I take it all back! I resign from this!"

But the judge said, *"Oh no!"*

Tom was arrested right then and there. He was convicted of purgery and submitting false evidence to the court, he was in jail for six months, *and* he lost visitation rights for two years.

When we got Micah back, he seemed groggy, like he had been sedated. We learned later that Tom had his truck packed and was ready to go. He and Micah had gotten their shots, their passports, and their plane tickets. They were going to leave the country—immediately after court.

If that woman hadn't done what she did, we probably never would have seen Micah again.

> *Avis knew Tom was a dangerous man; she'd heard the stories, and normally would have avoided him. But when he started boasting at work about what he was doing to his ex-wife ("I can just see DHS going into her house and pulling her nursing baby out of her arms as she screams...") she knew she had to do something.*
>
> *She called the Ventura County Courthouse to check if there really was a hearing. There was. So she feigned interest in Tom, invited him to her house, and offered him wine. Before the night was over, she had obtained his full confession on tape.*
>
> *She drove five hours to get to the courthouse.*
>
> *She was scared to death because she was certain Tom would try to take revenge (and he did), yet she willingly put herself in harm's way—to help total strangers—from the other side of the country.*

Jeanette: Even our lawyer thought this was divine intervention. He'd never seen anything like it.

Ken: Life is full of all kinds of injustices and unfair deals, but if people will just stop and invite the God of the universe into their lives, justice will be served. Sometimes it's on the other side of suffering, but justice *will* be served.

"For God shall bring every work into judgment, with every secret thing, whether it be good, or whether it be evil."
(Ecclesiastes 12:14 KJV)

And don't ever give in to your anger. The Lord *will* take care of things.

"Deliver my soul, O LORD, from lying lips, and from a deceitful tongue."
(Psalm 120:2 KJV)

"Dearly beloved, avenge not yourselves but rather give place unto wrath: for it is written, Vengeance is mine; I will repay, saith the Lord."
(Romans 12:19 KJV)

Distance
Ruthie's Story

I was raised in a Christian home, but as a young married woman, I found myself living a very sinful life, far from the Lord. Yet although I was keeping God at a distance, he was seeking to close the gap between us.

One day after work, I was walking to my car in front of my office, when I noticed a man up the street walking in my direction. The moment I saw him, I started rushing to get to my car. I don't know why; I'd never seen the man before, and he didn't look in the least bit threatening—but something in my heart told me to get away from him.

> **"Everyone who does evil hates the light, and will not come into the light for fear that his deeds will be exposed."**
> (John 3:20-21 NIV)

He was at least a hundred yards up the street, and I was only twenty-five feet from my car, but when I opened the door and turned to sit, he was there, right in front of me. As I stared at him, he calmly asked, "Are you walking with the Lord?"

I snapped at him. "No! I'm *running* with the Lord!"

"Are you sure?" he asked very gently.

"*Yes!*" I said, jumping into the car and slamming the door. But when I looked up, he was gone. I looked all around, he was nowhere to be seen.

At first I just thought it was weird that a stranger would come up and ask me about God, but when I talked to my husband about the incident, I began to realize that he couldn't have been an ordinary man. There was no way he could have traveled the distance of a hundred yards in a few seconds, and it was impossible for him to vanish the way he did; there was nowhere to hide. The whole thing really shook me up, and, as my husband and I talked, we both began to believe—that he must have been an angel.

After this incident I tried to fix myself. I did what I'd been trained my whole life to do. I started reading my Bible, I started praying, and I started going to church. But eventually I came to a place where I realized *I couldn't* fix myself, and I cried out to the Lord. "God, if you can't fix me, then I can't be fixed!"

The Lord was right there waiting for me. He forgave my sin, and I was filled with overwhelming joy and peace that I didn't know were possible. I became what the Bible calls a *new creation,* and, because of this, I was able to walk away from my sin.

By studying his word and walking closely with him, The Lord changed my life completely. He restored my marriage, renewed my love for my family, and has given me more blessings than I can count.

I now understand, that no matter how much distance I thought was between me and the Lord, he was right there beside me all the time.

> **"...For God has said,**
> **I will never leave you;**
> **I will never abandon you."**
> (Hebrews 13:5 GNB)

The Hiding Place
Herb and Flo's Story

> It is a pleasure to report
> on God's blessing of yesterday,
> how he supplied a need.

We moved to Houston, Texas, my wife Flo and I, in order that I might minister on behalf of Teen Challenge. For four years I was the director of Houston Teen Challenge. And you have to understand, I didn't make a lot. Flo and I learned to live on practically nothing.

When it became time, because of age and other things, for me to resign and head back up to Springfield, Missouri, we put our home up for sale, a nice house on a beautiful corner. But it didn't sell. For almost two months it didn't sell, and we couldn't understand it. Other houses in our area were selling in two to three weeks, but there were *absolutely* no buyers for our house. No one even looked at it.

We had around $19,000 in credit card bills and such, so we waited on the Lord to provide, and I went to work. I started working for a church, painting and doing carpentry work and so forth. And still the house didn't sell. So I told my wife, "Honey, take it easy. Don't pack too much, because we may still be here in the fall."

Then one day I received a telephone call from my wife. She said, "Honey, you'd better sit down for what I've got to tell you."

I said, "Alright."

She went on. "You know that door near the sink in the kitchen, the long, thin one where I keep my cookie tins and such?"

I said, "Yes."

"Well," she said, "I pulled all the tins out, and I pulled out all the dividers. Then I reached way in back to wipe down the shelf, and something came loose. It was a pink rag." She paused, then continued. "When I pulled it out—I found a roll of money."

"Go *on,*" I said.

"Then I pulled out the bottom drawer next to that cabinet, and found *another* roll of money. —Honey, I just found twenty *thousand* dollars!"

Naturally I went home.

I had to go see the provision God had made.

And wouldn't you know, the very next Saturday, the house sold, and with the help of that $20,000, we were able to leave Houston debt free. I paid off my $10,000 credit card for Teen Challenge; paid another bill for $9,000; tithed; and rented three U-Haul trucks to haul all of our belongings home. Back in Springfield we found a house in foreclosure, and were able to buy it outright. It was an unusual provision of God's grace and love.

And one more thing. When we bought our nice house on that beautiful corner in Houston, it had been sitting on the market for three *years.* Houses in that area generally sold in two to three *weeks.*

Whatever your experience may be,
you have a God who is just beyond that.
He is beyond the length of your problem.
No matter how much you may feel in the mullygrubs,
as they say down in Texas, that is not the end.
God is just beyond.

*"O the depth of the riches
both of the wisdom and knowledge of God!
How unsearchable are his judgments,
and his ways past finding out!"*
(Romans 11:33 KJV)

Teen Challenge is a Biblically based organization for drug addicts and alcoholics, which claims a 70-86% cure rate. Studies have supported this claim. In one study, 80% of the respondents credited developing a personal relationship with Jesus Christ as a major influence in helping them to stay off drugs.

Visit their web site at
www.teenchallengeusa.com,
or go to
http:/n.wikipedia.org
wikiTeen_Challenge
for more study results.

The Sobering Truth
Bob's Story

As I lay there staring out into that all consuming, complete, and total darkness, I heard a voice that said,
"This is what it's like without me."

As a third grader, I began my football career. I loved the game, I was good at it, and the coaches took a shine to me. For three years I played and was a happy kid, but then my little sister got very sick. She was born with cystic fibrosis, and at the age of eight, the disease attacked her body with a vengeance, and we lost her. This threw my family into an awful turmoil, and my parents split up.

My older brother turned to drugs, and at the age of twelve, I started drinking. When football season came around, I threw my heart and soul into the game because it gave me a sense of purpose, and it helped me forget my troubles, but when the season ended, I was empty. So as a sixth grader, I dove head first into the world of drugs. First my big brother introduced me to marijuana, then it was PCP, then mescaline, then opium.

I missed my eighth grade graduation because of an overdose, and in high school I had to pick my big brother up off the playground, in front of everyone, because he was passed out drunk. I had never been more ashamed or embarrassed in all my life, and I knew I needed to get away from that lifestyle, so I focused harder on football. But each year when football season was over, I found myself with a lot of time on my hands.

I wanted to get away from drugs, but I needed something to fill the void. So in my sophomore year, when my coach hooked me up with a weight lifting program, I gave it my all. Every day after school, I was in the weight room, working as hard as I could.

On New Years Eve, when I was fifteen years old, I told my brother I wasn't going to do drugs anymore. He laughed because he didn't think I could do it. But I did do it. I forsook everything, and focused on football and football alone. I wanted to be the best football player there ever was, and for the next two years, I kept my nose clean, I worked as hard as I could, and I made the All State team.

When Syracuse University offered me a full scholarship, I took it. But as soon as I got there I began to struggle. An offensive lineman was supposed to weigh 250 pounds or more—but no matter how many grueling hours I spent in the weight room, or how much I ate, I couldn't gain enough muscle mass to push me up over two-fifty. And if I didn't gain the weight, I would never make it to the pros. I was also struggling academically, so when I was given the opportunity to transfer to Rhode Island, which was smaller and closer to home, I took it.

I was more comfortable there, but as soon as I walked into the locker room, my eyes were opened to what was going on; the use of steroids was rampant! At first I was shocked, but the more I thought about it, the more I thought I'd found the answer to my problem. If I took this drug, I could gain the weight I needed, and if I gained the weight, I could make it to the pros. —I had told my brother I wasn't going to do drugs anymore—but this was something different.

I started taking steroids, and started increasing in size and strength. I got my weight up over two-fifty, and was playing better than ever. So when I read about the potential side effects, I paid no attention.

> *Among other things, anabolic steroid use in men can cause emotional problems, violent anger, accelerated baldness, impotence, trembling, swollen feet and ankles, jaundice, halitosis, aching joints, high blood pressure, kidney disorders, blood disorders, liver damage, and cancer.*

During my senior year at Rhode Island, I played so well that I made First Team All Conference. Then two NFL teams began recruiting me. I was tempted to go with the Dallas Cowboys, but ultimately chose the New England Patriots. When I arrived in Foxboro, I was still on steroids and had no trouble fitting in in terms of size and strength. I was given a trial as a free agent. Then one day I got a little taste of what it would be like to be famous.

In college, during summer breaks, I had worked as a camp counselor for the recreation department. The summer before my senior year, I had taken a group of kids on a field trip to see the New England Patriots. So now, as I was walking off the field with John Hannah (an All Pro and now a Hall of Fame offensive lineman), all of a sudden a large group of kids came running up to us. But they didn't want John's autograph, they wanted *mine!* They were my kids from the recreation department, and I was loving every minute of it!

For awhile it looked like I had a pretty good shot at making the team. I fit right in, I was playing well, and with my combined three lifts, I was the strongest rookie in the camp that year. But then I started to realize, I was just a tad bit slower than some of the other guys—and then I hurt my ankle.

The day I got cut from the Patriots was in late August. I remember it well. Dick Steinburg called me into his office and told me I could definitely fit into the league—but the Patriots simply didn't have room for me. I felt like somebody had died. It was the death of my vision, the death of my hope—so I went out and got as drunk as I could possibly get. It was the only way I knew how to kill the pain.

A short time later I got a call from a USFL team in Houston. They sent me airline tickets, but before I flew down for the tryouts, I was brought to see a prestigious doctor in a major Rhode Island hospital. Because I was a local hero, he was going to supply me with steroids. He called it a "necessary evil."

In Houston, steroid use was the worst I'd seen. Guys were walking around with bags of drugs in plain sight, shooting up in the locker room in front of everyone. I had always tried to hide the steroids, but these guys had no problem flaunting their "necessary evil."

I started trying out for the team and was making it to every practice, but, then afterwards, I would go back to the hotel and get drunk. Parties were ongoing, the night clubs let us in free, and people were always buying us food and drinks. At first I thought this was awesome, but as time went on, I realized if I stayed in football, I was going to end up seriously messed up—or dead. So I started praying every morning, "Lord give me the strength to keep on going, the wisdom to know right from wrong, and the courage to do the right thing." It was like a mantra, and I didn't really understand what I was saying, yet God was answering that prayer.

One night at a team meeting, I was sitting there

totally ripped from the drinks I'd consumed with dinner, when one of the guys stood up and announced there was going to be a Bible study on Thursday nights. A *Bible study*? That was an interesting concept. I didn't even know what a Bible study was. This guy was a respected player, the captain of the defense. He'd received All League Honors the year before. This guy seemed to have his life together, and I remember looking down at my hands, and thinking, *My* life is a *mess.*

One morning soon after this, I found myself looking in the mirror, and all I could say was, "God, get me out of here! I can't do this anymore."

I had a twenty-two inch neck, I could squat close to seven hundred pounds, and was benching about four hundred. I was a mass of strength—but an empty shell.

This time when I got called into the office for the bad news, I was okay. At the previous practice, I remember having my helmet on and thinking, *This is the last time I'm going to wear this thing.* I knew it was final, I'd had enough.

Soon after this, a friend hooked me up with a job in Maine as a teacher and coach at Bangor High School. I had vowed to myself, when I was cut from the team in Houston, that I wouldn't take steroids anymore, but I forgot one thing, I forgot I had to go through withdrawals. The doctor said it could take up to five years to get over withdrawals. It took me a year.

Trying to adjust to a new job, in a new state, while going through steroid withdrawals, was not easy. In seven months I lost sixty-six pounds, all the while feeling washed out, weak, exhausted—barely human. And it was difficult controlling my anger. One day a student mouthed off to me in the gym, and I shoved him hard through a curtain divider. I almost lost my job over that.

Within a few years of coming to Maine, I met and married my wife, Stephanie, and we had two boys. At one point we went to visit my mom and dad in Rhode Island, and we stopped in to see my old high school coach, Dennis O'Brien. He had always been like a second father to me, so when I heard he was diagnosed with terminal heart disease, I was anxious to see him.

During our visit I could tell something was very different about him. He was an Irish Catholic who had always been very committed—committed to smoking and drinking. I expected him to offer me a drink, but he didn't. Instead he looked at me from his chair, and said, "Bob, the best thing you can ever know is in this book." He was holding a Bible. He told me that he and his wife had started going to a Bible study. *A Bible study.* Again I was intrigued.

Dennis had stopped drinking, but for me, even though I had never gone back to drugs after the steroids, drinking was a different story. I'd started drinking when I was twelve years old, and after twenty years, it was still the only way I knew how to cope. Then when my brother died of an overdose in 1989, and my father died of leukemia in 1990, my drinking accelerated.

After these events, and a football coaching job that went sour, I got a job coaching with a man who had been a Green Beret in Vietnam. When there was time after practice, or on the bus, Don shared his story with me. He told about his experiences in the war, and how he had come back a total mess, but that the Lord had saved him. He was supposed to resign from coaching and move out of state, but he decided to stay on for one more year. Then when my anger once again landed me on the hot seat, he stood up for me. He said, "I believe the Lord wanted me to stay coaching one more year for Bob. The only reason I'm here is for Bob."

I was blown away! I didn't know what he was talking about! But he got me off the hook—then he invited me to a Bible study.

After several invites, I decided to go.

They were studying in the book of Romans, and as I sat listening, the verses began to grip my heart. I was a sinner. I deserved to go to hell. I immediately started thinking, *Where can I go? There's nowhere to hide. God is going to judge me.* But as I continued to listen, I learned how to receive forgiveness through Jesus who died for me. And I prayed for that forgiveness.

Immediately I began to notice a change in myself. During this period, I had been pursuing another love of mine, music. I'd been playing in a band for several years, and all of a sudden, some of the words in our songs became offensive to me. I didn't want to sing them anymore. God was changing me, but everything didn't change at once. I was still drinking. For three years I had drank at least a six pack every day, and went through one or two bottles of Jack Daniels a week. If we went somewhere where alcohol wasn't allowed, I hid a bottle in my pocket, so I could drink it in the bathroom.

One night at another Bible study another scripture gripped me. It's in Ephesians, and it says, "Don't be drunk with wine, but be filled with the Holy Spirit." This really got my attention, so I asked the guys to pray for me. I knew I needed to stop drinking, but I wasn't sure if I could do it on my own.

They prayed, and I stopped—for awhile. Then I went on a hunting trip with my in-laws, and when I got back to the camp before anyone else, I noticed a bottle of gin sitting on the shelf. I thought to myself, *I can have just one drink.* But then something snapped, and I finished the bottle, then stole my brother in-law's truck to go get more. That's all I remember.

They came and got me because they heard rounds being shot off in the woods. I don't remember the ride home, but I do remember my wife, she was *livid*. She had been at the end of her rope for some time, and I didn't even know it! She took one look at me, took the kids, and left.

I vaguely remember going downstairs to the kids room, lying on the bottom bunk, having bed spins, and falling asleep.

When I woke up, I was in total darkness. I knew I had a problem. My wife and kids were gone, and I couldn't stop drinking. For years I'd looked down on my brother because he was addicted to drugs, but there in the darkness, I realized, for the first time, that I was just as bad as he had been. I wanted to stop drinking, but I knew I couldn't do it on my own.

As I lay there staring out into that all consuming, complete, and total darkness, I heard a voice that said, **"This is what it's like without me."**

I cried. "I can't do it. —I don't want this. —I don't want darkness. —*I can't do this, Lord! I need your help! I can't stop drinking! Please help me!"*

After that night, I never had another drink. The Lord cured me. Right then and there I was healed. And I vowed in my heart that I would serve him.

> **"and call upon me in the day of trouble;
> I will deliver you, and you shall glorify me."**
> (Psalm 50:15 ESV)

There was a time when I sought fame because I thought it would satisfy, but today I know recognition is simply knowing that you are God's son or daughter. There was a time when I thought physical strength was the answer, but now I know real strength can only come from the Lord.

> *"For bodily exercise profits a little, but godliness is profitable to all things, having promise of the present life, and of that which is to come."*
> (1 Timothy 4:8 MKJV)

Because of my use of steroids, my joints are in very bad shape. A couple of years ago I had an MRI. The doctor said I have the knees of an eighty-five year old man. The cartilage is almost gone. It's almost bone on bone. This is not normal for a forty-three year old. A friend of mine from college played in the NFL for six years, and was on steroids much longer than I was. He died at thirty-eight from heart disease.

My advice to young people is to trust in the Lord, not in your own strength. Let God guide and direct you. When you have to train for something, give it all you've got, but give it over to God. If it is his will for your life, then he'll give it to you.

Any time I have difficulty I go back to the day I cried out in the darkness. That night, I learned something I will never forget. No matter how complete the darkness, it can never extinguish the light, and the only one who can take away spiritual darkness, is *The* Light.

> *"And cast ye the*
> *unprofitable servant into*
> *outer darkness: there shall be weeping*
> *and gnashing of teeth."*
> (Matthew 25:30 KJV)

> *"Then Jesus spoke again*
> *to them, saying, I am the Light*
> *of the world. He who follows Me*
> *shall not walk in darkness..."*
> (John 8:12 MKJV)

Stuck
Cathy's Story

Nine inches of fluff, and school was cancelled. So the boys and I were out playing, and I decided to take the snowmobile for a spin. I started it up and headed toward the hill, when suddenly I heard my son hollering behind me. *"Mom! MOM! Dad said NOT to drive the snowmobile down the hill! He said it would get stuck! —**MOM!**"*

I heard what he said, but my pride made me keep going. I thought, *No big deal. I know what I'm doing! I won't get stuck!* So I ignored him and headed on down the hill. At the bottom I began to turn, and *instantly* the machine was buried. I was *stuck!*

My son said he told me so, but I didn't want to hear it. *"Go get some shovels!"* I hollered up the hill. So my three boys and I started digging. We would dig—I'd start up the snowmobile—it would move a few inches—it would get stuck again. For *forty-five*-minutes we dug and pushed and pulled and tried everything we could think of to move that machine. And in forty-five minutes we moved that snowmobile *maybe* three feet. Finally I looked at the boys, and said, "You know what? We really should pray."

So we prayed. And then...

I started up the snowmobile, pressed the gas, and immediately drove 100 yards straight up the hill. Just like that! The kids were screaming and laughing. They knew it was the Lord! —What I learned from this experience: *Listen* to your husband, and when you get stuck, pray *FIRST!*

"...continuing instant in prayer."
(Romans 12:12)

Little Warrior
Eryn's Story

I saw a picture of my baby today. So far he just looks like a little blob, but I'm in love already. The doctor says everything looks good, and if the baby arrives on schedule, he or she will be born on April 13, 2004. Brian and I are happy, and Orianna is excited about having a baby brother or sister to play with. I've been having weird pains, but the doctor says it's nothing to worry about.

I'm about half way to my due date, and the baby's kicking a lot now. Orianna is so funny. Every day she comes up to me and wraps her arms around my belly. First she kisses it on one side, then on the other, and then in the middle. It's the cutest thing. She can hardly wait to meet the baby.

I'm worried because the pain I've been having since I got pregnant hasn't gone away like everyone said it would. I'm twenty-five weeks along and I still have bad cramps every day. It's bearable but it worries me. I want to have another ultrasound to make sure the baby's okay, but since my first pregnancy was normal, and my insurance won't cover another ultrasound, the doctor sees no reason for it. —We still don't know if we're having a boy or a girl. Brian wants to know, but I want to be surprised. And we haven't agreed on a name if it's a boy. If it's a girl we'll name her Evangelina, after Brian's grandmother, but I don't feel at peace with it being a girl. I believe this baby is a little boy, and I want to name him Jeshua, but Brian doesn't like it and he's hated every other name I've suggested.

I'm six weeks away from the baby's due date. The pain has never fully gone away, and we still can't agree on a boy's name. Today I looked through a book of baby names and still didn't find anything, but when I put the book down, the name Wyatt popped into my head. It sounds perfect to me, but I know Brian will hate it, so I won't say anything.

Yesterday I thought of the name Wyatt, and this morning, before Brian's feet even hit the floor, he said to me, "Honey, what do you think of the name Wyatt?" Now I'm sure we're having a boy because the Lord has given us his name. I'd like to find out what it means.

Brian's son Noah is hoping the baby will be born on his birthday which is March, 30th. I keep telling him the baby is due April 13th, and that there is no *way* I am going to have him two weeks early. But he keeps bugging me about it. He wants us to name the baby after him if it's a boy and if he's born on his birthday. I told him not to hold his breath.

I'm over eight months pregnant, and the doctor says the baby should have turned by now, he should be pointing downward. But I can feel his head constantly pressing up underneath my rib cage. It's *very* uncomfortable. No matter what position I get into it still hurts. The doctor finally scheduled another ultrasound. I'll go in on Thursday, March 26th.

It was exciting to see the picture of the baby. Those machines are just the coolest things. Orianna came in with us, and her eyes lit up when she saw the baby on the screen.

After the ultrasound Brian went out into the hallway to talk to the technician. I think he was asking about the sex of the baby. We've waited this long! Can't he wait a couple more weeks? Besides I know I am having a boy—and I can't wait to meet him.

—We are completely devastated—I don't know which way is up. My doctor told us the reason the baby hasn't turned is because he has something called hydrocephalus. I've never even heard that word before! I don't know what to think! The doctor said something about his head being too large because of water on the brain, and that something might be wrong with his heart! It's possible he might not live very long. He's going to send me to a specialist on Tuesday. We've finally stopped crying enough to get on the phone and ask people to pray. Brian is talking to Justin Alfred in California right now…

We stayed up almost all night praying and calling people. I might have slept for an hour or two. I woke up at 3:00 and heard Brian say, "Lord, if you wanted to get my attention, you've got it!" I don't think he slept at all. Last night we got on line and looked up hydrocephalus. One site had this awful picture of a little baby with a huge disfigured head. It looked like an alien! I can't shake the image from my mind. I wish we hadn't looked at it! My head is swimming. I just don't know what to do. Orianna keeps asking us what's wrong, but we don't know what to tell her.

We've called everyone we can think of, asking them to pray for the baby. I haven't slept much in the last couple of days, and I'm supposed to go in to see the specialist tomorrow to get a better idea of what's going on. —Despite everything, I know God is in control. —It's a few hours later, and I just got off the phone with my doctor. It's even worse than we thought. He reviewed the ultrasound, and they can't find one of the baby's kidneys! He doesn't know if staying inside the womb is good or bad for him. I have no idea what we're facing. —I might give birth to a dead baby. —I just don't know. —The waiting is killing me.

It's March 30th, and I'm heading to the hospital to see the specialist. I'm very tired, but I know the Lord is with us. I know a lot of people are praying.

They did another ultrasound at 10:30, and we waited until noon to hear the results. The specialist said the baby has the worst case of hydrocephalus he has ever seen, and he doesn't know how long he'll live. —He said it could be a couple of hours or maybe as long as a couple of months. They want to do an amniocentesis on me. They're going to stick a needle through my abdomen and take out some of the amniotic fluid to check it. I'm scared to do it—but I'll do anything if it will help the baby.

They want to do the amnio at 2:30, so I'm home making calls for Orianna to be picked up from school. I called her and told her I love her, and that she might spend the night with her friend because Mommy has to go for a test in the hospital. She was okay with that. She's been amazingly good these last few days considering the circumstances. It's hard to believe she's only six. We're going to have a quick prayer, and then head straight back to the hospital.

When we got here, they took us right up to labor

and delivery, and by four o'clock they finished the amniocentesis. It was horrible! I don't ever want to do *that* again! I've started having contractions, and they have me hooked up to a monitor to see how strong they are. They're starting to get worse, so I probably won't be able to write for a while. It looks like this baby isn't going to wait two more weeks to be born.

It's the next day, and I'm still in shock. Yesterday at 5:30 my contractions were getting worse, and the doctor came in and said they were going to go ahead and deliver the baby. I asked him when, and he said, "*Right now*." It all happened so fast. I didn't have time to do anything. Except pray. At 6:00, they said they were going to deliver him, at 6:15, they brought in blues for Brian, at 6:30 they prepped me for the caesarian, and at 7:11, Wyatt was born.

I'm in a lot of pain. I hurt all over. Everything happened *so* fast, it's all just a blur. They cleaned him up. I heard him cry once. He was wrapped up tight in a blanket, and I only got to see him for a minute. He has the sweetest little face I have ever seen. He was all pink and cute, and then they whisked him away to the Neonatal Intensive Care Unit. I didn't even get to hold him. Later on they wheeled my bed into the NICU, so I could see him. It was so hard not to be able to just pick up my baby and hold him. —I've had no time to prepare for all of this. I thought I was going to have a baby two weeks from now on April 13th, but I ended up having him on March 30th, Noah's birthday! He was right after all. I asked Brian if we could name the baby Wyatt Jeshua, and he said, "Well we have to put Noah in there too." So his name is Wyatt Jeshua Noah. Now Brian has two sons born on the same day, twenty-one years apart.

Today Wyatt is one day old, and they let me hold him for the first time. He weighs seven pounds, four ounces, and is seventeen and a half inches long. His head is larger than normal, but I think he's just perfect. He's so cute! They want to do a shunt operation on him tomorrow. They will put a tube inside his body, from his head to his abdomen, to drain the fluid off his brain. We're praying he won't suffer, and that the operation will be a success. I'm still exhausted and in a tremendous amount of pain, but I am focused on Wyatt. I've tried nursing him, but he just isn't into it. The lactation consultant came in and tried to help me, but I kicked her out. I know what I'm doing. I nursed Orianna without any problems. If Wyatt is going to nurse, he'll nurse, otherwise we'll just enjoy being close, and I'll pump my milk, so he can have it anyway.

The neurosurgeon came in to talk to us about the shunt surgery, but what he said wasn't matching up with what the doctor told us earlier. When he saw we were confused, he said, "Don't you know?" And we said, "Don't we know *what?*" He was irritated, and went out and told our doctor he needed to tell us what was going on. Then we were told Wyatt has something called holoprosencephaly. He said only half of Wyatt's brain formed, and basically Wyatt doesn't have a brain! He said Wyatt may never do anything, that he may be a vegetable for as long as he lives! They didn't give us any hope. But I'm not ready to give up yet. —God can do anything!

We just found a verse in Romans that gives us hope. The doctor said Wyatt doesn't have a brain. Well God can fix it if he wants to. Romans 4:17 says "… This happened because Abraham believed in the God who brings the dead back to life and who brings into existence what didn't exist before." If God wants to make Wyatt whole, he can do it.

It's Thursday morning, and Wyatt is two days old. I went in and held him and prayed. I want God's will to be done, whatever that might be, but I don't want to lose him! My friend called last night and said Pastor Ken told the congregation about Wyatt, and that they prayed for us. Ken came in just after Wyatt was born and prayed with us too. People have already started showing up with cards and words of encouragement. I know the Lord is in control. He can do anything. If he wants to heal Wyatt, he will heal Wyatt, if not, then we will take it one day at a time.

Several people have joined us for prayer while the surgery is going on. They will cut a hole in Wyatt's head and string a tube under his skin from his head down to his abdomen, where the fluid will drain and be absorbed into his body. One of the nurses printed some information about holoprosencephaly. These words are so foreign to me. I hope Wyatt isn't in any pain. He's so tiny. Lord Jesus, please let him be okay.

They had to stop the surgery. Apparently Wyatt has pulmonary hypertension, which means that his oxygen and heart rate are unstable. When they gave him the anesthesia, he couldn't handle it, his lungs filled up with fluid. They put a tube down his throat, so he could breathe, but when they took it out, he was struggling so hard, they had to "re-intubate" him, they had to put the tube back down his throat. So now he's worse off than before.

He didn't do well over the weekend. At the team

meeting they didn't come right out and say it, but they were asking us if we wanted to let him go, to stop treatment and just let him die! *They've* given up on him already! Well *I* won't give up! I said, "If you're asking me to pull the plug, I'm not God and I don't have that choice!" I can't *believe* they would even ask us that!

Wyatt opened his eyes for the first time in three days. The trauma to his body, and the medication put him out for awhile, but he's doing better today.

Lord Jesus, I lift this baby up to you and I thank you for blessing me with this precious little boy. I love you so much, and I know you love Wyatt more than I possibly ever could. I know you have a divine plan, and I know your ways are not my ways, nor are my thoughts your thoughts. Father, I pray for a tremendous miracle if it be your will. Just creating Wyatt has been a miracle. Now I'm begging that you would heal him.

Wyatt is six days old, and they need to discharge me. But they're letting me stay in the room until they need it for someone else. I'm glad because I can't imagine leaving Wyatt alone. He still has the breathing tube down his throat and a feeding tube in his nose. I'm still pumping so he can have mother's milk.

Today the doctor told me they're going to do the shunt surgery again on Monday, April 12th. And the social worker told me they need my room. They gave me an hour's notice. So I packed up my things, brought everything home, and came right back again. I'm feeling very stressed right now, very tense. I'm praying for peace.

When the social worker told me they needed the room, it scared me. I thought maybe they were just doing it because they don't want me around any more. Oh God please take this anxiety away from me.

Today is April 13th, Wyatt's due date, but instead he is two weeks old. Yesterday they did the shunt surgery, and it was a success! A bunch of people from church came to pray with us. The hospital let us use one of the conference rooms, which was nice. He seems to be doing well. He's resting comfortably.

I'm happy to have another day with my sweet little guy. Linda, one of Wyatt's nurses, asked me if I'd like to get some hand and foot prints. I said, "YES! What a great idea!" We made some prints on paper and put some in the front cover of my prayer journal. They came out really nice. You can even see the imprint of the little Band Aids on his tiny heels. He has the cutest little feet in the whole world!

It's two days after the surgery, and Wyatt's shunt is slipping out. They have to operate *again*. This is very frustrating. I just want Wyatt stabilized, so I can bring him home. This is my constant prayer. I will do whatever it takes to bring him home.

I held Wyatt for four hours straight today. The nurses said, "Why don't you go home and take a break?" But I told them no. I just wanted to keep looking at his beautiful little face. He has my nose and ears and maybe my mouth. He has his father's toes and fingers. He is a combination of the two of us, and I just love him. I feel totally blessed to be the mother of this little baby boy, and I pray God will mold me into the mother he wants me to be.

They fixed the shunt. Jeanette and a few others came in and sat with me during the operation. The doctor said it looks good. We'll see.

They did another CT scan, and it still wasn't working. It was still poking out! So they went in again, and this time they finally got it right. I'm getting frustrated with the doctors. —But I need to just give it over to God. *He* is in control. I need to stop and pray and know that even though I don't understand why all this is happening, he will get me through it.

Today was a good day. Wyatt's doing well, and I have a free cel phone! I told Tonya it was hard to get errands done because when I go home I want to stay right at the house in case the hospital calls. Tonya told her coworkers at Unicel about me, and they all wanted to help. They passed the hat, and today she brought in a gift basket, some money, and a free cel phone! What a blessing!

Wyatt's shunt is working, but because of the pressure in his head he's starting to have seizures, so they put him on phenobarbital. He's had the breathing tube for two weeks now, and they're going to take it out to see if he can breathe on his own. If he can do it we will be one step closer to going home.

I am so mad right now I could just …! It was time for rounds, so Dad and I had to leave. I knew they were planning on extubating Wyatt at some point. I talked to

Wyatt's doctor and told him I did *not* want Wyatt to suffer. I told him if Wyatt couldn't breathe on his own, I wanted him to be reintubated *right away*. He said he'd pass it along to the doctor coming on the next shift, but he didn't! Dad and I were sitting outside the maternity ward, waiting for rounds to be over, when a nurse came out and said they were looking for me. When we went in, Wyatt was doing awful! He couldn't breathe! His eyes were big and black, and his skin was gray! It looked like he'd been struggling for a *long* time! The doctor wanted to know what I wanted to do! No one had told her anything! I told her I could stand there all night trying to comfort him, but I wasn't going to. I said, "Get that tube in his mouth NOW! I don't want to wait!" And I walked out! They didn't need to let him suffer! They could easily have found me! They had my cel phone number! They could have paged me in the hospital! I don't ever want to see my baby like that again! There was absolutely no need for that!

It's Thursday, April 22$^{nd.}$ Wyatt is three weeks old. They did another MRI, and now the doctor tells us Wyatt *doesn't* have holoprosencephaly, but that he has something called an absent corpus callosum. They think the messenger box that allows the two sides of his brain to communicate is *missing*. So they said, sorry we made you learn about holoprosencephaly, he doesn't have it, he has this other thing. —I am *not* gaining any confidence in these people.

We had another team meeting today. I asked if it would be possible for Wyatt to have a tracheostomy, a permanent breathing tube in his neck. One of the doctors said he would NEVER be a candidate for a trache. He said it was not an option. So I let the matter drop. But I haven't given up on the idea.

I am so mortified right now! One of the nurses in the NICU told me, if I wanted to, they could just give Wyatt some medicine and "let him go quietly."! I said, "How could you even say that to me! I'm NOT going to do *that!*" Then she asked me what his quality of life would be! I still can't believe she said that! I don't even want her touching Wyatt! Obviously she's done! It seems like no matter what we tell them it's never a good enough answer. We are going to do what it takes to bring Wyatt home and give him the best life possible! The hospital wants us to pull the plug. I know they do! They say they're on our side, and that they support us, but then they keep questioning us! What do you want to do? What do you want to do? WE WANT TO DO WHATEVER IT TAKES TO GET THIS BABY HOME! When the Lord is ready to take Wyatt he'll take him, but it's not up to us to decide.

This morning I came across a verse in my Bible. It's Second Chronicles 20:12. It says, "For we have no power against this great multitude that is coming against us; nor do we know what to do, but our eyes are upon you." That is what I am focusing on right now. No matter what happens, or who may be against us, my eyes are focused on the Lord. He is in control, not the hospital.

Wyatt's primary day nurse is a good woman. She's honest with us and makes sure we know exactly what's going on, but she's also supportive. Today she confided in me. She told me about a little boy like Wyatt, only his parents couldn't handle it, and they abandoned him! His name was Alex. All of the nurses took him in as their own.

A foster mother was found for him. She loved him but he never made it out of the hospital. He never got off the ventilator, and he died. I can't stop thinking about him. How could a parent ever abandon their baby? I've been looking at the other moms in the hospital. I don't know how they do it without the Lord. I know the only reason I can do this is because the Lord is right here with me.

I've been told they're going to try one more time to extubate Wyatt. If he isn't able to breathe on his own, they're sending us to Boston. There's nothing else they can do here.

Today is Friday, May 7th. Wyatt is five and a half weeks old. He went for ten hours today without the breathing tube, with no luck. I held his hand and sang to him all day. He tried so hard, but he just can't do it. We're going to try one more time on Sunday, and if it doesn't work, we're going to Boston.

Well Wyatt didn't wait until Sunday. He pulled the tube out all by himself on Saturday. He went for several hours without it and didn't do any better than the first time, so we'll be heading out on the 11th. And guess what he's going down for? A tracheostomy, the thing they said he would NEVER be a candidate for.

It's Tuesday, May 11th, and I'm on my way to Boston. We left at 1:30 in the morning and we're almost there. They won't let me ride in the ambulance, so a bunch of my friends offered to take me down. It's been a quiet ride. I talked for a little while to Holly, but Jen, Sarah, and Marcy are trying to sleep. We're not supposed to follow the ambulance, but they stopped at the same rest stop, and we've passed each other a few times. We should arrive at about the same time. I don't understand why they wouldn't let me ride in the ambulance. This is stupid.

    Back home, one of Wyatt's doctors said if Wyatt got a trache, he would still be on the ventilator, and would have to live the rest of his life in the hospital. Well, Wyatt had his tracheostomy, and guess what? A half an hour later he was taken off the ventilator, and he hasn't needed to go back on it! I am so proud of him! I thank God for each breath he takes.

BREATH

As a breath finally escapes from his small smooth mouth
The mist of the breath is in the air

As I breathe in
I wonder

Am I tasting a bit of his breath
Which is now becoming my own?

It seems so simple, breath
Like something so uncomplicated

But to a baby who is taking his first
It can seem so miraculous

So when you go to take your next
Remember that if it weren't so,
Neither would you be so

He's only been in this world for seven weeks, and among other things, Wyatt has had four shunt surgeries, a tracheostomy, two MRIs, several CT scans, several x-rays, three EEGs, several echo grams, lots of ultrasounds, and many, *many* kisses! At this hospital they are checking him out from head to toe.

Wyatt has NORMAL brain tissue!! The doctors tell me he has severe hydrocephalus, but that he *doesn't* have holoprosencephaly *or* an absent corpus callosum. They think the fluid on his brain pushed his brain so far back against his skull that the doctors at home couldn't see it, but now they can see it! And it's *normal!* This is huge! The verse in Romans says God can bring into existence that which didn't exist before. That verse came true! They said he didn't have a brain, and now it's there! God can do anything!

The tracheostomy was a success. I'm happy about that, but now his shunt is ripping open and starting to poke through his head. I can see the white tube sticking out. They have to assume that it's contaminated and take the whole thing out, so they're putting in a new one tonight. I'm praying this will be the last time. Since these doctors have more experience, I'm hoping they can figure out what's going wrong and make it right once and for all.

Well it didn't get done, and now it's the weekend. For some reason they can't do shunt operations on the weekend, so they had to put him on an externalized drain. Now he has a tube that goes from his head to a bag next to his bed. He has to be kept at just the right level. If he's too high it will drain too fast. If he's too low it will drain too slowly. On a positive note, he hasn't been having seizures.

It's Saturday, May 22nd. They gave Wyatt morphine, and he stopped breathing *seven* times in the last 24 hours! Every time he stopped, they had to bag him to get him breathing again. I don't *ever* want him to go through that again!

A week and a half has gone by. They said they were going to do the shunt on Monday, but on Monday we got bumped to Wednesday, and on Wednesday they said they couldn't do it until Friday! They keep thanking me for being so patient, but I'm getting frustrated. The externalized drain is *highly* serious. There's a high risk of infection, and it shouldn't be left in any longer than it absolutely has to be. He's supposed to go in for surgery on Wednesday, May 26th—if we don't get bumped again.

My nerves are right on edge. It is *so* loud in this hospital. I'm having a really hard time comforting Wyatt with all this noise going on. I don't know if he is in distress, but he won't settle down, and the noise is driving me crazy!

Dear Father, I pray that, in a miraculous way, you would quiet the noise and let Wyatt hear only your music. The louder it gets the more upset I get. I need to pump, and I need to know Wyatt will be okay if I leave for awhile. Lord I pray for all of these babies and their parents. I pray for baby Sarah, Matthew, Jacob, Joshua, and this baby across from us who is always crying. You know his name. I don't know his name, but I know he is fighting because I hear his pain. Please give us your peace. Please give us your comfort and quiet, so that Wyatt will fall asleep and rest in your arms.

    I've been talking to Brian and things aren't going well. He doesn't think it would be a good idea to bring the baby home. At first he was with me all the way, but now he's having personal problems that need to be dealt with. He's going away for awhile. Orianna is going to stay with some friends…

    So much is happening here and at home that sometimes my mind just can't take it anymore. But when I turn to prayer and God's word, he comforts me. Earlier while I was reading my Bible, I came across a verse in John that says, "When Jesus heard that, he said, This sickness is not unto death, but for the glory of God, that the Son of God might be glorified thereby."

Voice inside my head
Question, thoughts of things people have said
My mind searches for answers
Wonders at why this could be

But the moment that I start that
Is when I stop being me
Me is the question of who I really am
The answer to that one is a Christian 'til the end

The end is endless because of my faith
To know that I'll be in heaven and not in this place
So while I am here and questioning the rules
My spirit reminds me of salvation and the tools

Which are the reminders in each day that passes
To keep God in the center and the rest in the wings
To be present in the moment, focus on the things above
Never question, never turn from the one true love

I thank God for his passion and commitment to me
I thank God for his faithfulness and love overflowing
through me
I thank God for his strength and his mercy and his grace
I thank God for bringing me to this place

For showing me that his power is greater than any other
That he loves me and cares for me like no other
Thank him for the child that he has blessed me with
And the strength that he has given him to make it through
the day

I know that his plan is greater than I can fathom
And I know that his love larger than I can imagine
He gives life to this child and grace to him too
He is constantly pouring mercy on us through and through

I pray that his plan is one I can understand
But even if I don't, he will help to comprehend
That his purpose is for his glory
And that I can understand

Well, Wyatt finally had the surgery they've been putting off, but instead of putting in a new shunt, they did an endoscopic third ventriculostomy, which should allow him to be shunt free. They think he had aqueductal stenosis, which means that the reservoir, where the fluid drains out of the head into the spine, was clogged. If the surgery is successful, then the fluid will drain naturally! That would be wonderful! I'm so glad these doctors are willing to go ahead and try different things to help Wyatt. The neurosurgeon even came and spoke to me personally to let me know the surgery went well. Praise the Lord.

Wyatt just had the worst seizure I have ever seen. It scared me! I hope it doesn't happen again. They did an eye and hearing test on him. He failed both tests. But what did they expect so soon after major surgery? Before the surgery when they flashed a light in his eyes he would squint, but now he doesn't. It seems like a part of him is gone.

Today Evelyn came to visit me from Calvary Chapel, Fitchburg. What a wonderful friend! She brought a great big gift basket and some money from the church. I can use the money; everything is so expensive here. I don't know where I'd be without the church helping us out. Even people who don't know me from a hole in the wall want to help us. Pastor Steve from the Calvary Chapel in the city visited me last week, and Pastor George Small from the Fitchburg church is supposed to be coming sometime. God is good.

Because of the externalized drain, it's been almost two weeks since I held Wyatt. But I come in every day and sit with him for hours. He has a private room now. They put a cot in here, so I can cuddle up beside him. I hold his hand and stroke his head. Sometimes I sing or read or play his CDs. We have a Comfort CD and one with harp music. The nurses finally stopped telling me to take a break. They understand that I want to be here.

It was so great to be able to hold my baby again! They took the externalized drain out of his head, and I held him for four hours straight. But then he started to feel a little warm, so I put him back in his bed and took his temperature. He had a fever of 101. They took some samples, and they're going to do a CT scan.

He has what's called basilis meningitis. Somehow, bacteria got into his cerebrospinal fluid (CFS for short). They think the Ventriculostomy didn't work, so the CFS isn't draining, but they can't put in a shunt until the infection is gone, so they have to put him back on the externalized drain. They've started him on intense antibiotics. They tried to put a catheter into his leg to administer the medication, but it wasn't working, so they had to put one directly into his heart. It's called a broviac line.

—It looks like we're going to be here awhile.

I've been running low on cash, but the Lord has provided. Someone at home found out I needed money and put $80 in my account. I also found a piece of glass in my food. When the hospital found out about it they apologized and gave me a $50 gift certificate. I can use it in the cafeteria or coffee shops.

Wyatt's been lying on his left side for the last eighteen days because of the externalized shunt. He's been on antibiotics for several days, but he *still* has the infection, and he's still having seizures. One of his nurses said it's important to keep them under control, but then another one said it's okay to let them happen! I got a third opinion and was told they definitely need to be kept under control, so I made it clear I wanted *all* the staff told that Wyatt's seizures need to be kept under control. I don't want anyone letting Wyatt suffer when it can be stopped.

Dad and Orianna came for a visit. The social worker got us a room at the Beacon House, and Jord came, and we all went out to eat. Dad was happy because he had both of his kids together. I didn't like being so far away from Wyatt, but it was great to see my family. Before they left we walked down to the swan boats and took a ride in one of them. Orianna *loved* that.

I want her to stay here at the hospital, but they won't let her stay in the family room with me. HELLO! It's called the *family* room. They offered to set us up at the Beacon House, and have Ori go into the daycare. But I don't have the money, I don't know the day care providers, and what's the point if she can't be with me? Hopefully I won't be here much longer. If only Wyatt would stabilize enough to have the shunt put back in.

Wyatt's numbers have been off the charts! They still aren't stable, but they're going to go ahead and put the shunt in. They don't want to wait any longer because of the risk of further infection with the externalized drain. They're going to operate today. We've been here for six weeks. I want to go home.

The surgery went well. If nothing else happens, we're going home in one week. This time they're going to let me ride in the ambulance.

Wyatt is stable, and we're going home tomorrow! I got to spend some more time with my brother today. I've only seen him a couple of times in the last two years, so it's been good to see him. He came down, and we drove over near the North end and walked along the water and had dinner together. I'm happy I got the chance to reconnect with him, but I'll be happier to get home!

We're on our way home! I don't get to ride in the back, but the nurse taking care of Wyatt is a good one. He's worked with him before. I almost can't believe we are finally going home. We spent *seven* weeks in Boston! It was only supposed to be a few days. I can't wait to see everyone. It will be so good to be home!

I didn't tell Orianna we were coming home because I wanted to surprise her. Tonya met us at the hospital. Wyatt's bed was decorated with balloons and welcome home signs. That was really nice. Then we went to Kelly and Garth's, and I snuck upstairs to where Orianna was. I poked my head in the door, and she just kind of looked at me, and said, "Mommy?" Then she ran and threw her arms around me and didn't want to let go. She was *very* surprised. It was cool.

They did a test on Wyatt to see if he's able to swallow. They gave him some disgusting milky liquid and then used a kind of x-ray machine to watch the white stuff go through his system. He did a good job swallowing, and it didn't go into his trache tube, but he couldn't do it fast enough. So they've scheduled him for another operation. They're going to put a feeding tube directly into his stomach, so he won't have to be fed through the tube in his nose anymore.

Wyatt's operation is tomorrow, and I suddenly have a high fever, so I can't be near him until it goes away! I'm freaking out because I'm sick, and I want to be with him for the surgery! I called the church. Ruthie's going to come and sit with him for the operation.

The last few months have been an emotional roller coaster. First they said he might not live. Then they said he had no brain. Then they said he had no corpus callosum and that he would never get off the ventilator and that he would die in the hospital! But guess what! He *has* a brain. He *has* a corpus callosum. He *is* off the ventilator. And he's coming home! My little baby has defied them all. He has refused to give up, and against all odds we're going home!

I told the doctors in the last team meeting, "You never gave me any hope, you never encouraged me, all you did was tell me we could let him go. The nurses told me, the nurse practitioner told me... everyone thought we should let him go. No one encouraged me." They were surprised, and said they never meant to take my hope away. Apparently they've had a lot of parents accuse them of *not* warning them about the worst that might happen. So now they always make sure they tell people the worst. They apologized for not being more encouraging.

Wyatt has started having episodes, and no one can figure out what's going on. We need to find out what this is before we can go home.

It's been a month since I last wrote. We're going

back down to Boston. They found a growth called a granuloma formed in Wyatt's trache. He'll need to have it removed. They're going to put in a longer pediatric trache. That should take care of the problem.

This morning Wyatt's nurse, Mary, looked at me with tears in her eyes. She sees that no matter what happens I am *not* going to give up. She said if *anyone* is going to get Wyatt home, it will be me. She told me I am a one of a kind mom, and she believes I can make it happen. I *can* make it happen, if it's God's will. I can do all things through Christ who strengthens me!

I was a little worried going down to Boston because of what happened last time, but everything went well, and we were only there a couple of days. It was nice to see all the familiar faces, but I'm glad to be on the way home.

It's Labor Day, so a friend and I took Orianna to the fair. But the hospital called, and we had to leave. When I got back here he was on the ventilator. I'm spending the night in the hospital because he is so sick. No one can figure out what happened … —I know what happened. One of the nurses down in Boston had a bad cold. She *never* should have been around the babies. Wyatt ended up being on the ventilator for a week and a half, and now that he's off. He has a blood infection. —Will it never end?

It's September 21st. Two more weeks have passed. The blood infection is gone, and the doctors are talking about sending Wyatt home again. They've started training me on his home care. If all goes well he will come home on September 30th.

During the team meeting, the doctor who's been so negative looked at me, and said, "You know, you don't have to bring him home, there are other places he can go." I wanted to just yell at him, "GIVE ME A BREAK! When are you going to say, hats off to you?" Why can't they just give credit where credit is due? I want my baby *home* with me. Is that so hard to understand?

Against all odds, my boy is coming home!

Wyatt is home! Thank God Wyatt is finally home! It is September 30th, 2004. Wyatt is six months old today. My dad is here with the video camera. He got it all on tape. Now he's waiting for Orianna to get home from school, so he can catch her reaction on film. It is so wonderful to finally have him home!

It's been over six months since Wyatt came home from the hospital. He's getting stronger all the time, and he does something new every day. He's learned to give kisses, and sometimes he smiles. He likes holding on to the bars of his crib, and he's learning how to sit and hold his head up.

It's been a challenge becoming a single mom, because Brian is gone for good, but there are many people helping us. From Shelly at the fire station, who helped me install Wyatt's special car seat, to the ladies at the church, who continue to bring meals every week. One lady who's a friend of a friend gave me $500 just when I needed it, and I've found envelopes with money several times. People don't want credit, they just want to bless us. Orianna got to go to horse camp for free, and friends bring her to and from school every day. The Lord knows what we need and has continued to provide.

My dad has been a huge help. He's learned Wyatt's care, so I can get out of the house or take a nap. He's helped us financially and emotionally, and he's been good to talk to about Wyatt because twenty-two years ago he spent time in the NICU with my little brother . —And he always makes me think about the hard questions like, "Are you keeping Wyatt alive for Wyatt, or are you doing it for yourself?"

Orianna adores her little brother. Sometimes it's hard because she's no longer the center of attention. I know she wants to go out and hang out with Mommy the way we used to, but she understands that right now, Wyatt has to come first. She's been so brave, and I think God is preparing her for something.

Wyatt has a nurse who comes in for 28 hours each week. Marie is absolutely wonderful. Sometimes I think she loves Wyatt more than I do! I don't know what I would do without her.

And finally, I am thankful to God. Without him, I wouldn't have made it. James 4:8 says if you draw near to God, he will draw near to you. Daily I have sought him, and he has never left us. Many people say they can feel the Lord's presence here, I think he and Wyatt have something worked out between them. My dad thinks Wyatt is not here for himself, but that he's here for us—to teach us something—to show us something. I don't fully understand what Wyatt's purpose is yet, but God knows the end from the beginning, and I trust him.

I know I may not have Wyatt forever. I've told him many times if he wants to go home and be with his Father, it's alright. I know it would hurt. It's the hardest thing to say, but I know I'd be alright. —But God hasn't taken him yet, and until he does I will continue to love Wyatt every day. This is my journey. It's what the Lord has given me, and I can either say 'No thank you,' or I can embrace it. And I am embracing it.

Wyatt has a shunt, a feeding tube, and a trache. We're not sure if he can see or hear. His seizures have become infantile spasms. He needs twenty-four hour care, but he's worth it. I look at him and I see the most beautiful little boy in the whole world. He has the most amazing brilliant blue eyes and the most perfect little lips. He's *so* cute. The Lord has blessed him with this awesome cuteness. He's always cuddly, and I *never* think anything negative about him. I never think *why am I doing this?* Sometimes people say to me, "Oh it must be so hard…" but is it hard to love somebody? Is it hard to care for someone you love? No. I love him. He's my little boy—and he's perfect.

Wyatt is the strongest little person I have ever known. The doctors had to open his head up fifteen times in a three month period. He's had five different internalized shunts. He's endured thirty-three surgeries, several bouts of infection, numerous seizures and a host of other complications. They said he might not make it a week, but he's still here and he is over a year old.

No matter how many prayers were said, or how much *I* wanted him to live he would have died if *he* had given up the fight. But he hasn't given up. He is a tough little guy, who has bravely faced each and every battle. He has fought for his life over and over again and tasted sweet victory each and every time! He's my little trooper, my courageous little soldier.

Before he was born God gave this little boy his name. And by the way, the name Wyatt—it means Little Warrior.

"Before I formed you in the womb, I knew you..."
(Jeremiah 1:5 GW)

Jesus said,
"When I was hungry, you gave me something to eat, and when I was thirsty, you gave me something to drink... When I was sick, you took care of me..." Then the ones who pleased the Lord will ask, "When did we give you something to eat or drink?...or visit you while you were sick...?" The king will answer, "Whenever you did it for any of my people, no matter how unimportant they seemed, you did it for me."
(Mat 25:35-37,39-40 CEV)

When Wyatt was four years old, it was discovered that his shunt wasn't draining properly. Tests revealed that it was completely clogged, but that Wyatt's cranial pressure was registering at twelve, which is normal. The doctor was very puzzled at this. Wyatt's mom said, "So you're saying it's a miracle that his shunt failed, and his body figured out another way to reroute the fluid." The doctor didn't disagree and continued to look very puzzled, unable to explain what had happened. This was over a year and a half ago, and Wyatt has been shunt free ever since!

Wyatt with big sister, Orianna.

Jolted
Dave's Story

I've been a long-haul truck driver for thirty-four years, and only once do I remember falling asleep at the wheel. Well, I don't actually remember falling asleep, but I will never forget waking up.

It was back in the late 1980's, and I was doing a route I had done many times before. Starting from Maine, I had traveled down along the eastern seaboard to New Jersey where I stopped to unload and pick up another trailer. From there I would drive through the night to reach my next stop outside of Boston at 8:00 a.m. It was a hard trip, but I was used to doing it, and normally I had no trouble staying awake.

However, on this night, I was *tired*. I just could not keep my eyes open—and I nodded off. But before the truck went off the road, something jolted me awake. I was holding the wheel when something, or some*one*, touched me on the back of my left hand, and it was no ordinary touch. It felt as though someone's finger went right inside the back of my hand. Suddenly I was WIDE awake, and I remember saying, "Lord, you've got my attention!"

My hand went completely numb for six or eight hours, and I certainly had no trouble staying awake for the rest of the trip!

I guess there are all kinds of ways for God, or one of his angels, to get your attention.

> ***"Therefore let us not sleep, as do others;***
> ***but let us watch and be sober."***
> (1 Thesalonians 5:6 KJV)

Katahdin
Jamie's Story

Earlier in the day, I had slipped and fallen,
and now I was petrified that I would slip again
because now there was nothing there to catch me.

    We had never climbed Mount Katahdin before, so we didn't realize just how *long* it was going to take. When we reached the summit (5,267 feet above sea level), we had been hiking for over eight hours, and it was already four in the afternoon. That meant we had barely four and a half hours to make it back down to the base of the mountain before darkness overtook us. So we took a quick break and asked someone to take our picture, then with legs still shaking from the climb, my husband, my eighteen-year-old son, my sixteen-year-old daughter, and I began the long descent back to the base of the mountain.

    After a couple of hours of scrambling backwards down over rocks and ladders, we reached the plateau near Thoreau Springs, and paused to have a look around. From here we could see the trail for a good distance above and below, and we took note that there was no one in sight in either direction. We filled our water bottles and moved on.

    About an hour later we reached the area called Gateway (I call it *the gateway to HELL*) where the narrow pathway begins precariously winding its way along the top of sheer cliff areas. I, for one, was *terrified!* Earlier in the day I had slipped and fallen backwards against some rocks. Now I was *petrified* that I would slip again because now, there was nothing there to catch me.

    With my son taking the lead, and my husband

bringing up the rear, we began scooting and crawling along the dangerous pathway. Shaking with exhaustion and gripped with panic, we inched our way along. At first we were dead silent, but then my voice broke through the quiet. "Oh GOD, *please* get us off this mountain! *Please* get us off this mountain!... " Over and over again, I pleaded for help.

And the light began to dim.

Suddenly, out of nowhere, another hiker appeared behind us. We didn't see him coming. We didn't *hear* him coming. He was just there. And without saying a word, he began to help us. We made room for him to get by, but instead of moving on, he stayed with us for over an hour, helping us get over the rough spots, one—step—at a time.

As the path got a little easier we, had the opportunity to talk and get a better look at the man. His name was Steve, and he appeared to be in his late fifties. He was of medium build; his clothing looked like that of any other hiker; but his eyes were *so* blue, a pristine blue—and very deep. He talked about family, and he told us that he hiked the mountain every weekend. He also told us he was a teacher.

At one point on the trail, we encountered another hiker, sitting on the ground in distress. Steve asked if he was okay, and the man told him he had run out of water. We were almost out of water ourselves, but Steve pulled out a brand new sealed bottle of water, and gave it to the man.

When we reached the tree line, we parted company, and he was gone, just like that.

And as we carefully picked our way through the darkness at the end of the trail, my husband spoke words that I will never forget. He said, "You know, God sent that angel to help us."

I said, "I know."

We are deeply convinced that God heard our prayers and sent us a helper. If that kind teacher hadn't shown up, we would have been forced to spend the night on the mountain, completely unprepared, without sufficient food or water, and without shelter. There is no doubt in my mind, that that man was an angel—if not the Lord himself.

> *"...the LORD will certainly have pity on you when you cry for help. As soon as he hears you, he will answer you."*
> (Isaiah 30:19 GW)

> *"The LORD may give you troubles and hardships. But your teacher will no longer be hidden from you. You will see your teacher with your own eyes."*
> (Isaiah 30:19-20 GW)

At the top of Katahdin

Our Daily Bread
Laura's Story

Now it isn't unheard of for us to be invited out to dinner, but three times in one week?

  My husband's job provides enough income so I can stay home with our two children, but there are times when we run out of money and have to call on God to provide. So far he has never let us down.
  One October I managed to get the bills paid on time, but there was nothing left to buy groceries, and we wouldn't get another paycheck for two weeks. I could have held back on the tithe, the ten percent we give back to God, and used that money for groceries, but I didn't do that. And I didn't waste a single moment worrying about it; God is always faithful to provide—and I think he really enjoys finding cool ways to give us what we need.
  Now it isn't unheard of for us to be invited out to dinner, but three times in one week? On Monday night we had roast chicken, carrots, green beans, and mashed potatoes with gravy at my parents' house. On Tuesday night we had spaghetti and the worlds' *best* meatballs at a friends house. On Wednesday eight bags of groceries miraculously appeared on our front steps. And on Thursday my cousin Kathy invited us out to Pat's Pizza for some *seriously* greasy pizza. (But if you mop up the grease with a pile of napkins, it's *awesome*. Really.)
  So just as I knew he would, God provided enough food for us to get through until the next paycheck, but he didn't do it the way I thought he did. *I* thought my friend, the one who made the worlds' best meatballs, was the one

who brought us the groceries, because she was the *only* person I'd told about our food situation. But when I thanked her for the groceries, she told me *she* didn't buy them.

My next thought was that she must have called the church, and someone from there had deposited eight bags of groceries, hit the doorbell, and sprinted back to their car (a light green four door), so they could speed off without being identified. But my friend told me she hadn't called the church either. She told me she had been at home minding her own business, when some friends showed up with groceries. They thought she could use them, but she didn't need groceries. So she told them our address, and they brought the groceries to our house. They didn't want to know who we were, and they didn't want us to know who they were. They knew if they did a good deed in secret, God would reward them openly.

> **"...so that your merciful deeds may be in secret. And your Father who sees in secret Himself shall reward you openly."**
> (Matthew 6: 3-4 MKJV)

> **"The LORD will not allow the righteous soul to famish,..."**
> (Proverbs 10:3 KJV)

> **"So do not worry, saying, 'What shall we eat?' or 'What shall we drink?' ...But seek first his kingdom and his righteousness, and all these things will be given to you as well."**
> (Matthew 6:31-33 NIV)

The Cross
Larry's Story

I started to cross before I saw it,
a little black car *flying* around the curve at a breakneck
speed... I had just enough time to form one thought.
She's got me.

  I think I've had a protector all my life. When I was three years old, I was run over by a big black car. There were tire marks all down my sleeve, but I was unharmed. When I was a little older, I was hit two winters in a row, on the same street, by the same man, in the same car. The first time I ended up unconscious in a snow bank, but both times I walked away with only a few minor scratches.

  In the Navy I found myself in plenty of dangerous situations, but I was never seriously hurt. One time when I was stressed out and worrying, some unseen person spoke words of comfort to me. I had just put in for retirement, I was in Hawaii, and there was no way for me to go on job interviews in the states. I was walking around in my flight suit starting to panic, thinking, *What am I going to do? How am I going to support my family?* when clear as a bell, I heard a voice say, "God's going to take care of you. Don't worry."

  But of all the times I've been protected, the following incident is the most amazing.

  It was the winter of 1991, I was at a safety conference in Brunswick, Maine, and I had come down with a nasty cold. My head was throbbing, so when the instructor called for a break, I took the opportunity to run down the block to the drugstore. I needed some Tylenol.

I walked down to the intersection, and paused. It was a busy, two lane, one-way street which curved out of sight. In the near lane the traffic was stopped for the light, but the far lane was clear, so I crossed between two vehicles in the first lane and slowed to look up the road. Nothing was coming.

What happened next is permanently etched in my memory.

I continued my stride out into the second lane, when all of a sudden a little black car came *flying* around the curve at a breakneck speed. At a distance of about twenty-five feet, impact was imminent. There was no time to react. There was nowhere to go. I had just enough time to form one thought. *She's got me.*

In reflex I began to step back—but then something unexplainable happened. I found myself surrounded by a cocoon of warm peace and protection, then instantly I was back beside the car in the first lane, and the little black car bumped the side of my knee. I was not afraid. I was not shaken up. In fact, I don't even think my heart rate went up.

The woman in the car was frantic.

I walked around the car. She rolled down the window, and I calmly asked her, "Are you okay?" She was a wreck, she was beside herself crying, so I gently told her, "It's alright. I'm okay. You didn't hit me."

In the Navy I'd been in a lot of situations where I'd ended up having the shakes. So when I walked into the drugstore, I remember thinking, *The shakes are going to hit me any minute.* But they never did.

I've been around machinery all my life. I've seen enough to know if something is moving as fast as that little car was moving, there's no way it can stop in twenty-five feet. And I know how fast *I* can move. There was no

possible way for me to get out of the way of that car.
It wasn't luck, because there's no such thing as luck.
I think I've had a protector all my life.
And the peace and protection I experienced—something like that can only come from God.

*Jesus said, "Peace I leave with you,
My peace I give to you... Let not your heart
be troubled, neither let it be afraid."*
(John 14:27 MKJV)

*"For surely, O LORD, you bless
the righteous; you surround them with
your favor as with a shield."*
(Psalm 5:12 NIV)

Erika's Angels
Julie's Story

We would fly through the air to get a hand under her head. "Don't let her fall!" was like a mantra.

Viola Williams didn't like me very much, or at least I didn't think so. She was the only African American woman in our office, and she was a loner. For days she wouldn't even acknowledge me, but then strangely enough, she would leave a little gift on my desk, and there would always be a Bible verse attached. In fact, when she did talk to me, she was always quoting scripture.

And like this wasn't weird enough, when I was nearing my due date with Erika, she asked if she could come to the hospital when I went into labor. I tried to discourage her; I barely knew the woman. But she was insistent, and ultimately I agreed to let her come.

I was in labor for fifteen hours, and Viola stayed at the hospital the entire time—praying. She sat out in the waiting room until my husband needed a break, then she'd come into the delivery room. She'd lay her hands on my leg and pray under her breath, and I remember thinking, *What's the big deal? People have babies every day!* My pregnancy had been perfectly normal. I just couldn't understand what all the praying was about.

When Erika was delivered, Viola was *thrilled*. Anyone would have thought it was her baby the way she carried on. And this was very unlike her, since she was usually so reserved.

Four months later we found out, babies like Erika, usually die during childbirth, or shortly thereafter.

> ***"...pray one for another, that ye may be healed. The effectual fervent prayer of a righteous man availeth much"***
> (James 5:16 KJV)

First her belly button didn't heal, then her forearm swelled up for no apparent reason. She got bruises just from sitting in her car seat, and broken blood vessels in her mouth just from sucking. And sometimes there was blood in her stool. The doctors in North Carolina were at a loss, but when we moved home to Maine, her new doctor was determined to find out what was wrong. Two months later Erika was diagnosed with an extremely rare form of hemophilia called Factor VII Deficiency.

Hemophilia is a hereditary blood disorder in which a person has a deficiency or absence of certain clotting factors in their blood. In order to contract the disease both parents have to be carriers. Symptoms of hemophilia can include; excessive bleeding, excessive bruising, nose bleeds, and abnormal menstrual bleeding. A person with hemophilia runs the risk of developing joint disease, vision loss, anemia, or neurological problems. Major blood loss, or bleeding in a critical area, such as the brain, can be fatal.

In the United States, there are approximately 18,000 people with hemophilia, but the large majority have Factor VIII or Factor IX Deficiency. Factor

> *VII Deficiency is almost unheard of. There are only twenty to thirty people alive in the United States today, who have Factor VII Deficiency.*

Very little information was available, and what the doctor did find was all bad. We didn't know what to think. We had no idea we were carriers. All we knew was that our baby girl had a deadly condition, and that there was no available treatment in the U.S.

My supervisor's wife was a nurse, and as soon as she heard of Erika's diagnosis, she went to the hospital library and photocopied everything she could find on Factor VII Deficiency. But what she found was very bleak. In every case study the child had ended up dying. She found nothing that offered even a glimmer of hope, so she didn't want to give me the photocopies, she thought I was better off not knowing.

Two weeks later her husband put an envelope on my desk. He indicated there was nothing hopeful inside, but he wanted me to have it anyway, because he thought I had a right to know.

I didn't want to open it. I didn't think I could take any more bad news, so I let it sit there. *I won't read it. Not now. Not here. I'll wait until the weekend, when I have time to cry.*

But something kept nagging at my heart. I *needed* to read it. I didn't want to, but I felt compelled, so I picked up the envelope. There were pages of medical jargon, most of which I didn't understand, but one case study stood out to me. It was about an infant who had died of a brain hemorrhage—and one of the symptoms he'd displayed was a bulging soft spot.

That night, Erika had a brain hemorrhage.

It was May 8, 1990. In the middle of the night, Erika started crying and vomiting, so I immediately called the doctor and described what was going on. When I asked about a brain hemorrhage, he said if she wasn't having seizures, then a brain hemorrhage was unlikely. He told me to give her Pedialite, and to call him back in two hours. But after hanging up the phone, I remembered the case study and put my hand on my baby's head. Immediately I called the doctor again. Erika's soft spot was bulging.

At the ER they diagnosed a brain hemorrhage and started giving Erika fresh frozen plasma to build up the clotting factor in her blood. We had to wait four *long* hours until it was safe to operate, and the doctors told us she *wasn't* going to make it. But she *did* make it! They were able to operate in time, and she pulled through.

If I had waited two hours and then called back, Erika would have died. But because I had read *that* case study *that* day, she survived. It was a miracle. There's no doubt in my mind.

> *As time went on, treatment was found for Erika. Because of spontaneous bleeds, usually deep in a muscle, she needed to have a shot of Factor VII concentrate every other day. Growing up, Erika rarely had spontaneous bleeds, but the threat of an accident and subsequent blood loss was always a constant concern.*

Erika's first step was both exciting and terrifying, all at the same time. And, *"Don't let her fall!"* became like a mantra. If she stumbled, we would *fly* through the air to get a hand under her head before she hit the ground.

Miraculously, she learned to walk without any major accidents, but there was no time to relax—because then she started *running*. She would fly around the house, and time after time, we'd see her veer straight towards a door casing—but she never hit one. Never! We were forever in awe and amazement, looking at each other saying, "How did *that* happen?" We were sure she was going to smash right into a sharp corner, but somehow she would cruise right by, just missing it.

She must have had more than one guardian angel.

She doesn't remember these early days, but she does remember one near accident when she was five.

Erika: I was playing bat and ball with my dad. I was only five, and he was trying to throw it so I could hit it. But this one time he threw it too far, and then he turned to go back towards our garage.

The ball went over my head, and when I reached up with the bat, my foot slipped, and I started to fall backwards. I thought I was going to land on my head on the pavement, and it really scared me! I can remember thinking, *If I hit the ground, this is going to be bad!*

But then all of a sudden, I stopped falling. I felt a hand on my back steadying me. It was a large hand, like a big man's hand, and there was a tingling feeling, like something was giving me strength. I was tipping way back, but it held me there until I got my balance, and then I stood up. I looked around—but there was no one there. So I ran into the garage yelling, "Mom! Dad! An angel helped me!"

I had never fallen that hard before, so thinking about hitting my head on the pavement, and then feeling myself being pushed back up... it was God! I don't know how else to say it!

> *"For he will command his angels concerning you to guard you in all your ways; they will lift you up in their hands..."*
> (Psalm 91: 11-12 NIV)

> *"Behold, I send an Angel before you, to keep you in the way, and to bring you to the place which I have prepared."*
> (Exodus 23:20 MKJV)

****

At five months of age, when she had her brain hemorrhage, Erika's right frontal lobe was disabled. At two and a half, she lost the vision in her right eye. Today, at fifteen, she has a spontaneous bleed somewhere in her body approximately once every ten to fourteen days. She can't play sports. She can't jump rope. She can't roller blade. She's tried these things, and they all cause bleeding. Yet she is the most optimistic person I know.

She is always an encouragement, I think because she herself has been through so much, and when someone is having problems, she really *listens* and never fails to direct them to prayer, often praying with them right there on the spot.

Each and every day Erika continues to be a bright spot in our lives. Her wit is quick and her laughter abundant. Her love for young and old is evident in the flash of her brilliant smile. Not only is she a miracle, she is truly a blessing from above.

<u>Some of Erika's favorite verses:</u>

*"For I know the thoughts
that I think toward you, saith the LORD,
thoughts of peace, and not of evil,
to give you an expected end."*
(Jeremiah 29:11 KJV)

*"always giving thanks
for all things to God the Father in the
name of our Lord Jesus Christ,"*
(Ephesians 5:20 MKJV)

*"Trust in the LORD with all
your heart, and do not lean on your own
understanding. In all your ways acknowledge
him, and he will make straight your paths."*
(Proverbs 3:5-6 ESV)

Pierced
Nancy's Story

I wanted to get up and take the bread, but I wasn't allowed. I slouched down and peeked up at the people waiting in line. In the whole church, only three others were still sitting. To me, not being able to take the bread, meant that I wasn't good enough.

They told me God loved me—but I wasn't convinced.

I tried smoking pot when I was twelve.
By fourteen, I was getting high every day.
I dressed to get the boys attention.
At fifteen, I was sexually abused.
I tried cocaine... and acid...
and started bingeing and purging.
But nothing filled the emptiness.

When I was still in high school, I moved in with my boyfriend. Rob was good to me at first, but it wasn't long before he started abusing me. I put up with it for several months, but the night he ripped the phone out of the wall and sent me to the hospital with a ruptured eardrum, I'd had enough. The next day I moved back home.

Then I met another man. Gary was fun loving, and we both loved to party, so it made perfect sense to move in with him, but then *he* started abusing me. At first it was only with words, but after I got pregnant and decided to keep the baby, the abuse began to get worse.

I had quit smoking and drinking after getting pregnant, but I would still go out to the bars with Gary.

Then one night when we got home after he had been drinking heavily, I said something that made him mad, and he shoved me hard. I shoved him back, and the next thing I knew, I was on the floor with him on top of my pregnant belly. This sent me into labor.

So again I moved home. And even though Gary and I tried to reconcile for the sake of our child, we never did get back together again.

After Brooke was born, I became overwhelmed with the responsibilities of being a single mom (and with life in general) so I started smoking pot again. Then my bingeing and purging got so bad, the purging became easy, I barely had to try at all to make it happen.

I knew I had a problem, so I sought professional help and was diagnosed with Attention Deficit Disorder and depression. My doctor put me on depression medication so I would stop binging and purging. He also suggested I see a therapist.

I thought the therapist would tell me to stop smoking pot. But he didn't. He told me, in my case, smoking pot was actually *good* for me! He said it had a calming effect on my ADD, and he saw no reason for me to stop.

In three years, I saw a psychiatrist, a nutritionist, a Master of Social Work, a psychologist, and a Licensed Clinical Social Worker. I was put on Paxil, Prozac, Welbutrin, Zoloft, Buspar, and a mood stabilizer. But each of these drugs only masked my feelings—and caused side effects. The pull to the refrigerator and the need to get into an altered state were still there. So I continued to drink, and binge, and smoke pot...

At the age of twenty-one, I completed beauty school, then managed to get a job and a place of my own.

However, I still craved attention and a sense of belonging, so I was always looking for a "good" man. Then I met Matt. At first he was fun, but early on he became very controlling and suspicious. I never moved in with him, but the whole time we were seeing each other, he was sure I was cheating on him. So after awhile, I told him I didn't want to see him anymore, but he wouldn't leave me alone.

Then one day, while cutting a woman's hair, I began telling her about this ex-boyfriend who was harassing me. I felt I could open up to her because she was different. She would always ask how I was doing and how my daughter was, and she was always very interested in what I had to say. So I started telling her about Matt because I thought maybe she would sympathize, but instead she started quoting things from the Bible! I stood there trying to maintain my composure; I couldn't *believe* what she was saying. She told me what *God* had to say about me, and even suggested that I had brought my problems on myself by the way I was living. How dare she say I was "living in sin!" What a whack job! This time, when I finished her hair, I was glad to see her leave.

But then she came back and did it again! What a Froot Loop! Time and time again she came back, and it got to the point that whenever I saw the name Ann in the appointment book, I *dreaded* her coming. Didn't she know it wasn't okay to talk about religion in public? Clearly this woman was just a little bit *off,* but what could I do? I couldn't say anything because we were taught in beauty school to *never* talk about religion or politics with clients.

So I was polite to her, but I wasn't going to change the way I was living for her sake. If I wanted to "live in sin" and binge and smoke pot (hey, the "professional" told me it was alright), then that's what I was going to do!

Nothing she had to say about *God* was going to change anything. Besides, God probably didn't love me anyway; I was never allowed to take the bread.

Then one day I dropped Brooke off at the sitter's and decided to go out for a walk before getting ready for work. When I got back, I went into the bathroom and turned on my curling iron—then nearly had a heart attack when Matt stepped out from behind the shower curtain!

I *screamed* at him to get out, but he *demanded* to know where I had been and who I was seeing. We started shoving each other, and the next thing I knew, I was on the floor with his hands around my throat. I couldn't breathe! I flailed my arms and legs. Then I guess he realized what he was doing because he loosened his grip, and I somehow managed to get up and grab my hot curling iron. When he came screaming at me again, I warned him, but he kept coming, so I hit him on the face with the iron. Then he smashed his fist against my ear. I kept screaming at him to get out and to get out of my life! Finally he took the hint and stormed out.

I probably would have called in sick, but I was the new assistant manager; I *had* to go to work. When I got there, my ear was still swollen, and I was still shaking, and who should be there but Bob, the nut case's husband. He saw how upset I was and started asking questions. I ended up crying and telling him everything.

The next day Ann showed up. This time she didn't just tell me what God had to say about me, she actually took her Bible out of her bag and started pointing out scriptures! In my head, I was thinking, "Oh *great,* here we go again!" But in my spirit, the words just *pierced* through me.

> ***"Know ye not that the unrighteous
> shall not inherit the kingdom of God?
> Be not deceived: neither fornicators, nor
> idolaters, nor adulterers, nor effeminate, nor
> abusers of themselves with mankind, nor
> thieves, nor covetous, nor drunkards,
> nor revilers, nor extortioners, shall
> inherit the kingdom of God."***
> (1 Corinthians 6:9-10 KJV)

I knew what she was showing me was the truth. But then I met Brian. He was perfect! He had his own business, he loved my daughter, he loved to party—and he loved me. Who could be more perfect? So after taking it slow at first, we rented an apartment together. I wanted to buy a house so I could start my own salon, and I thought maybe we could save up and buy a house together.

Then Ann started inviting me to church. After awhile, even though I still thought she was different, I decided to go. I went with her a few times, then one Easter Sunday when the pastor asked if anyone wanted to accept Jesus as their Savior and have their sins forgiven—I raised my hand. *Finally,* I got to take the bread, *The* Bread, The Bread of Life. Jesus.

> *"Jesus said, "I am the living bread...If anyone
> eats of this bread, he will live forever. This bread is my
> flesh, which I will give for the life of the world." ... "The
> spirit gives life; the flesh counts for nothing. The words I
> have spoken to you are spirit and they are life."*
> (John 6:51; John 6:63)

At this point Ann bought me my very own Bible. And wasn't she excited! She also invited me to a women's retreat in Cape Cod. My spirit had come alive, and I now felt a hunger for something else. Something more. So I went to the retreat and roomed with the "nut case" and three of her friends. This was a real turning point in my life. I was baptized and I truly began to see the world through new eyes—and it was there in that room in Cape Cod that I learned what God's will is for his children. I also learned the importance of daily Bible reading, and that the Gospel of John was a good place to start.

Back at home, Brian said I changed right before his eyes. We would still go out, but it wasn't the same. I would still occasionally smoke pot, but now there was a sense of unrest about it. And even though I loved Brian, and he was good to me, I decided to trust what the Bible said about the way I was living, and I moved back in with my parents. I continued to see Brian, but something in my heart told me he wasn't the one for me.

Soon after this, Brian went to a school reunion and met an old girlfriend. Three months later they were married.

I continued to trust God and put into practice what I was reading in my Bible—and God started working miracles. A client of mine was selling a house that I desperately wanted to buy. It was the perfect size, in a nice area, and it even had room for a salon. But there was *no way* I could afford it. So I started going to the house and praying. I would park in the driveway and pray, then I got the keys and went inside and prayed some more. For over a month I prayed. And whenever I started feeling overwhelmed, I would recite this scripture because it brought me peace.

> ***"Be anxious about nothing,***
> ***but in everything by prayer and by***
> ***petition with thanksgivings, let your requests***
> ***be made know to God; and the peace of God***
> ***which surpasses all understanding will***
> ***keep your hearts and your minds***
> ***in Christ Jesus."***
> (Philippians 4:6-7 LITV)

On paper there was no way I could afford to buy the house. But I bought it anyway. I took a step of faith. I had exactly $517 in my savings account. The owners wanted only $500 down! And they were asking $711 a month to owner finance the house. This was far more than I could afford. But somehow, some way, every month I managed to pay the bills. Everything seemed to fall into place, and even the curtains I had bought for my apartment matched *perfectly* with the curtains already in the house. I knew God was answering my prayers!

First, against all odds and without the help of a man, I bought a house and started my own salon. Then, I started praying for a husband. "Lord, can you bring me someone who really loves me, loves Brooke as his own, and of course, loves you with all his heart? —And, oh yeah, it would be great if he could cook too."

Then I met Mike at church.

I will never forget the night I was looking in the mirror and praying about Mike. I felt the Lord say to my heart, "He is going to be your husband." And he was! He is! After so many failed attempts at relationships, I finally trusted God to show me who I should marry, and I am now married to a man who is good to me, who completes me.

And oh yeah, he used to be the head chef in a restaurant.

God was working in my life, and the more I trusted him, the more he healed me. I didn't have to clean up my act. I came as I was, and slowly he came in and began to clean my house, one room at a time.

After smoking pot almost every day for fourteen years, I was able to stop. After struggling with an eating disorder for more than ten years, I met Sandy and Kelly, two women who had struggled with the same problem. Whenever I was tempted to binge, I would call one of them, and they would pray with me. They helped me get through without the use of drugs.

I had finally come to a place where I *knew* that God loved me. I didn't need drugs, or alcohol, or food, or therapy, or anything else to fill the void. All I needed—was Jesus.

Mike and Nancy have been married for eight years and have added two children to their family. Their marriage has had many ups and downs, but God has been faithful to get them through the rough spots.

There have been times when Nancy was tempted, and fell back into old sinful habits. But she was quick to repent and turn back to the Lord for forgiveness and comfort. And he has never let her down.

> ***"... God is faithful,
> and he will not let you be tempted
> beyond your ability, but with the temptation
> he will also provide the way of escape,
> that you may be able to endure it."***
> (1 Corinthians 10:15 ESV)

I don't know where I'd be if Ann hadn't been so persistent. For close to two years, she and her family prayed for me. I resisted everything she had to say, I didn't want to listen. But when she took her Bible out of her bag and actually pointed out the words, they *pierced* through all my defenses.

> ***"For the Word of God is
> living and powerful and sharper
> than any two-edged sword, piercing even to the
> dividing apart of soul and spirit..."***
> (Hebrews 4:12 MKJV)

Now when I'm doing someone's hair, and they tell me their problems, I'm the one likely to pull my Bible out of my bag to tell them what *God* has to say about things.

Amy Carmichael of India once asked a stonecutter which blow of the hammer broke the stone. He answered, "The first, and the last—and every one in between."

So when you are speaking the truth in love (Eph. 4:15), don't become frustrated if you think nothing is happening. As the Spirit leads, just keep on hammering, because even though you may not be able to see it, just below the surface, the door to someone's heart may be opening.

> **"so shall My Word be,
> which goes out of My mouth;
> it shall not return to Me void,
> but it shall accomplish that
> which I please..."**
> (Isaiah 55:11 LITV)

Make It Blue
Stephanie's Story

One winter, when we were just barely getting by, our car died. So I prayed this prayer: "Dear Lord, we need a car, and we only have four hundred dollars. Could you make it a station wagon because we have four kids. And oh—could you make it blue?"

Three days later a Volvo station wagon appeared with a sign on it two houses down. It was for sale. It was $400. And it was blue.

"And all things,
whatever you shall ask in prayer,
believing, you shall receive."
(Matthew 21:22 MKJV)

Take My Hand
Sandy's Story

We wanted to have a baby right away. It didn't matter that we already had three beautiful girls from my first marriage to care for, we wanted a baby of our own, so I got pregnant right away.

At first the pregnancy was going along very well, but then something went very wrong. At the end of my first trimester, I started spotting and ended up having a miscarriage. Nothing like this had ever happened to me before, I had always become pregnant quickly, had easy pregnancies, and bore healthy babies. So the loss of this baby was *devastating,* and for weeks I grieved.

But after some time had passed, we were ready to try again, only this time, I went to the doctor first for a check up. He examined me, did a pap smear, and gave us the go ahead to try for another baby.

Five weeks later I received a notice in the mail. It was my test results. They weren't good. The pap had revealed "displaced cells" and I needed to call my doctor right away.

On the phone the nurse gave me information beyond what my mind was able to comprehend. There would have to be tests taken because this could be an indication of cervical cancer. She kept talking, "... cells... tests... biopsy... surgery... invasive... hysterectomy..."

But my mind had frozen up at the word cancer.

I went in, and they took tissue samples from my cervix for further testing. Results revealed that I had carcinoma in situ III, stage three of cervical cancer. Two thirds to the full thickness of my cervix was cancerous. And to make matters worse, it was likely that the cancer would soon reach my uterus, if it wasn't there already.

They also discovered—that I was pregnant.

The doctor wanted to do what's called a laser conization immediately. This would remove the cancerous part of my cervix and determine if the cancer had reached my uterus. It was imperative I do this right away to stop the cancer as soon as possible, BUT, it was also likely to cause another miscarriage. The doctor laid out our options. I could go ahead with the procedure and risk having a miscarriage; I could have an abortion, do the procedure, and get pregnant again after the cancer was dealt with; or I could go on with the pregnancy and be closely monitored to see if the cancer was spreading. This latter option would put both the baby *and* me at risk.

Taking the life of our child was not an option, and we were grieved the doctor would even suggest it. However, we understood the longer we waited, the more likely the cancer would become life threatening. If I had the test, I was risking the life of my baby, *but* if I didn't have the test, I was taking the chance of losing the baby *and* leaving my husband without a wife, and my three girls without a mother.

One of my neighbors was in nursing school, so I borrowed her books and read everything I could about my situation. What I read matched what the doctor was telling us; his urgency was justified. As much as we wanted this baby, we now began praying that God would take it away.

I began going in every few days for blood work, and the hormone indicating pregnancy, called HCG, was increasing with each test. This indicated a viable pregnancy. Again the doctor asked us to consider an abortion. Again we made it clear that abortion was not an option. And we continued to pray. Our church family at Calvary Baptist was praying, and our friends at Penobscot Christian School were praying. We even had people at a friend's church in Florida praying for us. All we wanted was for God to either bless the pregnancy—or take the child.

And I was at peace.

I had every reason to be stressed out and anxious, but as we continued to pray for God's guidance, there was peace.

Two weeks after my diagnosis, I woke up one morning and discovered that I was bleeding. When I miscarried the first time it was devastating, but this time there was a sense of elation. God had made his decision, and I knew everything was going to be fine.

That day my husband came with me to my appointment, and the doctor presented us with a D+C, a procedure to dilate my cervix and remove the inner lining of my uterus. This would speed up my recovery, so he could go ahead with the laser conization. My husband and I looked at each other. If there was any chance the baby was still alive and had a chance of surviving, we were not going to have anything to do with destroying it. But the doctor was insistent. He wanted to do the D+C on the spot. So we asked for some time to pray.

Our prayers were intense, and as we prayed, we both felt sure that it was okay to go on with the procedure. There was a complete peace about the decision; somehow we both knew that the baby was already gone.

The procedure was *excruciating*, and I realized as it went on, that it was the same procedure used to perform abortions. It was absolutely horrible! And it gave me a small glimpse of what women go through physically and emotionally when they have an abortion.

That being done, I was scheduled to come back in two weeks for the laser conization. But a few days later, a nurse called and said I needed to come in right away. I could tell by the tone of her voice that she was surprised at what she had to tell me. There wasn't a *trace* of chorionic (or HCG) found in my amniotic fluid when it was tested in the lab. Only a few hours had passed between when I'd started bleeding and when I'd had the D+C. There *should* have been chorionic in the fluid. Then the nurse told me, maybe the doctor "hadn't gotten it all."

The record was clear. My HCG levels had been increasing with each blood test, so there was no doubt that I had, in fact, been pregnant. And when I went in for another blood test, the HCG level had dropped significantly, indicating that the doctor *had* "gotten it all." So why wasn't there any HCG in my fluid?

A short time later, I was telling my story to a friend when suddenly I knew. There wasn't any chorionic in the fluid because God wanted to reassure us that the baby was gone before the D+C was performed. He wanted us to know beyond a shadow of a doubt that we did not have any part in taking our baby's life. Loud and clear, he was saying to me, "You did not take your baby. I did. When you seek me, and I take care of things, I am complete. I love you, and I am going to take care of you."

It still blows my mind every time I think about it.

The laser conization removed the cancer from my cervix, and the cancer had not reached my uterus. I was then declared cancer free.

A few months later I became pregnant with our daughter, Ashley.

> ***"...And the LORD shall guide
> thee continually..."***
> (Isaiah 58:9,11 KJV)

    While Ashley was still a baby, my husband was also diagnosed with cancer. For close to two years our lives were completely unpredictable with hospital visits, tests, and treatments, and it wasn't long before I found myself getting thoroughly stressed out.

    Then one day while walking through the hospital parking lot, Brittney, my five year old, refused to hold my hand. She was terrified that at any moment she was going to get hit by a car, but she would *not* hold my hand. I was frustrated with her stubbornness, and I remember thinking: *Why does she have to do everything herself! Why won't she just take my hand?* Then suddenly I realized something. *I* was doing the same thing with God! And I felt the Lord speak to my heart. *You're scared of things you can't control, but all you need to do is take MY hand, and I will guide you through.*

> ***"For I the LORD thy God
> will hold thy right hand, saying unto thee,
> Fear not; I will help thee.***
> (Isaiah 41:13 KJV)

    Soon after this, my husband was declared cancer free.

That Still Small Voice
Jean's Story

It was another wonderful ordinary day at my beloved camp. There I stood at my kitchen sink, washing dishes, and looking out the window at the trees gently moving in the wind. But my eyes kept returning to one tree in particular. It was right next to the driveway. My car was parked beside it.

That tree is going to fall.

What? That's dumb. Why would I think that? It doesn't look like it's going to fall. It's windy—but it's not *that* windy.

That tree is going to fall. You should move the car.

No. That's stupid.

Ten minutes passed, and the thought kept bugging me.

So I went out and backed my car up a few feet.

Twenty minutes later *that* tree fell in the driveway right where my car had been!

Immediately I thanked the Lord for saving my car.

My thoughts on this experience: That inner voice we sometimes hear should be *listened* to and taken *very* seriously!

"Be still, and know that I am God:..."
(Psalm 46:10 KJV)

The Nurse's Aide
Marie's Story

There are many miracles,
especially when a person puts all their faith in God.

The miracle that started my career as a nurse happened in 1971 when I realized I had to provide for my family. I had taught dance lessons before I was married, and then was a housewife with six children for many years, so my experience in the work force was extremely limited. My neighbor, an Italian woman, was also looking for work. She had plenty of experience but couldn't write English, so we decided to combine forces and help each other out.

The morning we were to start our job hunt, I went to mass and knelt at the altar. With total faith I asked Jesus to help me find a job.

First we went to St. Joseph Hospital, where I helped my neighbor fill out an application. Since she had spent many years working in a pizza parlor, she was hired on the spot to work in the kitchen. I, however, did not get a job; they were not going to hire someone with no experience. So I was a little disheartened, but then we moved on to the next place on our list, Downey Community Hospital. This time before we went in, I prayed, "Please, God, I need a job."

Now as a rule, when you enter any large hospital, there is a desk with volunteers who answer questions and help people find their way around. But at this hospital, we were greeted right at the door. The man looked to be around forty years old and he wanted to know if there was anything he could do to help us. I remember thinking how much he looked like my brother Maurice, except for his eyes. Maurice had brown eyes, but this man's eyes were very blue.

I told him, "I need a job. I have no experience because I've been a housewife for many years, but I'm willing to do anything, scrub floors, clean bathrooms, any menial job. Anything."

He led us to the back of the hospital, towards the right, and down a hallway to his office. Once there, he told me if I took classes to become a nurse's aide, he would give me a job. Then he called in his secretary, a very bashful lady who looked to be in her fifties. He asked her to find out where and when the nurse's aide class was going to be that night. She smiled sweetly at us, then went and did as he asked.

A few months later, after I was trained, the teacher took me aside and told me that I should put in an application at a certain hospital, and that I shouldn't tell anyone else about it. I did as she said, and I was hired, just like that!

At this point I went back to Downey Hospital to thank the man who had helped me, but when I asked about him at the desk, no one knew who I was talking about. I described him, telling them how tall he was and what he looked like, but they just looked at each other. They couldn't think of anyone who matched that description. I described the man's secretary. They didn't know who she was either. So I set out on my own to find his office, but I couldn't find it! I walked all over the place where I remembered it being. It just wasn't there.

They did have an employment office, but it was on a different floor.

I believe Jesus sent an angel to help me.

****

In 1977, I was working nights as an LVN (Licensed Vocational Nurse), and had started taking classes during the day to become an RN. It was very difficult, and I felt I was neglecting my home, so I decided to give it up. But before I quit, I went out to breakfast with another nurse, Mary Doolittle. She told me *not* to give up. She knew about a special class where, if you had three or four years of LVN experience, you could go and become an RN in only one year.

I went home and told my son Wade about this class. He said I should give it a try, but I didn't go right away. Then the next night while I was at work, Wade called me three times telling me I shouldn't put it off any longer, or the class would get filled up. He was very persistent.

I asked a co-worker to go with me, and we went the very next day to the college where Mary said the class was going to be. A group of people were coming out of a room, so we asked them where we needed to go to sign up for the class, and they were amazed. How did *we* know about the class? They had just found out about it themselves! They told us where to go, and we were the first ones to sign up.

The next day we were told that the class was only for LVNs at a different hospital, and our money was returned to us, but they said to call back later, and if anyone dropped out, they would make an exception and let us in. When we called later, five people had dropped out.

During the time when I was taking this class, Mary Doolittle asked me where I had heard about it. I told her, "YOU told me!"

She didn't remember.

I told Wade, "It's a good thing you kept calling me about signing up for this class, I almost missed the opportunity."

He said, "I never called you."

****

When my mother was still alive, it was very difficult finding private time with her, so occasionally we would buy McDonald's food for the kids and then go park the car in front of a little restaurant. We would go inside, sit by the front window, and have a quiet lunch together while watching the kids eat their lunch in the car. Well, one day we were doing this, and one of the kids released the emergency brake, and the car started rolling backwards towards the road! I bolted out the door, but before I got there, I saw a man, who looked like a truck driver, get behind the car and stop it. I jumped in the car and pulled up the emergency brake, but when I turned around to look, the man was gone. In a few seconds he had vanished.

Another time, there was a nurse at work who wanted to get even with me because I got the job she was trying to get. First she smashed my headlights. Then one day while I was driving on the freeway, a man in a car to my right started beeping his horn at me. He motioned that I should get off the freeway, and immediately I had a feeling that something was wrong, so I took the next exit. There was a tire store right there, and I stopped to have the car checked. They found two large staples in both of my back tires! If I had kept driving, I might have been involved in a major accident, putting my life and the lives of others in danger.

There was no way the man on the freeway could have known anything was wrong with my car.

Unless perhaps he was an angel.

*"The angel of the
LORD encampeth round
about them that fear him,
and delivereth them."*
(Psalm 34:7 KJV)

*"For he shall give his
angels charge over thee, to keep
thee in all thy ways."*
(Psalm 91:11 KJV)

A Simple Prayer
Autumn's Story

It was a frigid cold day deep in the heart of evergreen country, where a little girl stood holding her mama's hand in the snow covered driveway. The mama looked down at the little girl and made a sad face. "Honey, our van won't start, and we don't know why. Grampy doesn't know what's wrong with it, and Daddy doesn't either. Do you think we should ask God for help?"

The little girl looked up with big serious eyes, and nodded.

So the mama prayed. "God, our van won't start, and we don't have any money to get it fixed. You say, in the Bible, if we need something we should ask. Well, it sure would be nice to have our van working again. Please help us. In Jesus' name we pray…" She looked down and smiled at her little daughter, who finished the prayer.

"Am-en." (Which sounded more like, "I'm in.")

"Now won't it be fun to see how God fixes our van?"

A couple of days later the little girl's uncle (who had never been particularly concerned about other people's vehicles before) suddenly decided to do something. He commissioned the services of his mechanic friend, and together the two of them came and fixed the van right there in the driveway, in the rain. The uncle paid for the part, and the friend refused the offer to pay him later. He said he was just glad to help.

And the mama said as she strapped her little girl into her car seat, "Wasn't it fun to see how God answered our prayer? I never called a tow truck. I never called a mechanic. I never asked Uncle Kenny for help. I didn't make one phone call and I didn't spend a dime. All I did was say a simple prayer, and now our van is running perfectly again. Isn't God amazing?" She looked into the eyes of her little daughter and added, "Shouldn't we thank God for this blessing?"

The little girl nodded seriously.

So the mama prayed, "Dear Lord, thank you for giving us Uncle Kenny and his friend, Elliot, so our van could be fixed. It's really great to have our van running again. Thank you so much for all you do for us. In Jesus name we pray..."

The little girl snuggled down into her car seat, smiled, and said, "I'm in!"

Jesus said,
"... Truly, truly, I say to
you, whatever you shall ask
the Father in My name,
He will give you."
(John 16:23 MKJV)

Take My Life
Jeremiah's Story

"If there's a God who loves me, then he can have me.
I don't want my life anymore.
I don't want control anymore.
If I have control,
I'm going to kill myself."

My whole life I was looking for love in the wrong places. Humans want to be loved and we want to be needed. I wanted that feeling my whole life, maybe because my parents are divorced, maybe because I'm just messed up. I don't know.
Every Sunday, from as far back as I can remember, we went to church.
When I was ten, I started breaking into buildings.
My father was a narcotics officer.
When I was fourteen, I started selling drugs.
I was a bad kid.
By the time I finished high school, my criminal record included: petty theft, possession of drugs, and shoplifting, and this was only what they *caught* me doing. I was the guy people looked at and said, "He'll never amount to anything." I was the guy who would die of liver cancer by the time I was twenty-six. I was the guy who would end up in prison long before that.
My mother got me a good job in a hospital, but I was drinking every night and hungover every day. Then after I wrecked my new jeep and got a DUI, not only did I lose my vehicle, I lost my license, my job, and my house.
So I went to live in a fraternity. I never went to a

single class at Fresno State, but I lived there for a year and a half—because I could drink a lot. In fact, it got so bad, I started carrying a tape recorder in my chest pocket so I could remember what I'd done the night before.

Then I started doing a lot of drugs.

And one night I tried to kill myself.

But it didn't work.

I woke up the next morning curled up in a fetal position on the floor, crying. Vomit was everywhere. And I remember praying, "If there's a God who loves me, then he can have me! I don't want my life anymore. I don't want control anymore. If I have control, I'm going to kill myself!"

Jesus said,
***"For whosoever will
save his life shall lose it: but
whosoever will lose his life for my
sake, the same shall save it"***
(Luke 9:24 KJV)

That day there was a newsletter in the fraternity mailbox. It was from a Christian camp called Hume Lake, and it was addressed to me. This was weird, because no one had my address at the fraternity, and I had never gotten mail there before.

I'd gone to this camp as a sophomore in high school, so I was familiar with it. The newsletter said they were hiring, and something told me that I should apply. So I did.

When I got to the camp, I asked the ladies in the office, "How did I get here? Explain this to me please. How did I get this newsletter when no one has my address?"

They searched their files, but they couldn't find the address. I couldn't have gotten a newsletter from them.

They said it was impossible.

So I started thinking—Maybe there is a God.

I quit drugs and alcohol (since they weren't available) and I started working as a cashier at the camp diner. I had a lot of time in between customers, so I started reading the Bible, and one day I read something that sounded wrong. Jesus said he didn't come to bring peace, but a sword. *What? I thought Jesus wanted everybody to be friends! You know, peace on earth?* Then I read that he said to love your enemies, and if someone hits you, you should let them hit you again. *WHAT? No! If someone hits you, you hit them back!*

I had gone to church my whole life, but this was the first time I had ever read the Bible for myself. I didn't understand what Jesus was saying, but I wanted to know more, so I kept reading. Then one day I read that Jesus claimed to *be* God. He said in John 8, "...before Abraham was, I Am." So I started thinking, either Jesus was *completely* nuts—or he was actually God.

One day I had a day off and I wanted to go fishing. I didn't have a pole, and I didn't have any money, so I went to the office and asked the ladies if I could get an advance on my pay. They told me they couldn't do that. Then they asked if I had prayed about it.

I thought, *Prayed about it? You people are crazy! So what will happen? I'll PRAY for a fishing pole, and one will just SHOOT out of the wall? You and your Christian... WHATEVER! Did I PRAY about it? That's just so stupid! It's the dumbest thing I've ever heard.*

So I prayed about it. I did it out of spite, but I did it anyway. "God can I have a fishing pole? I really want to go fishing. It's nothing bad. I'm not doing drugs anymore. I'm not drinking. So can I at least have a fishing pole?"

When I got back to my trailer, my roommate came in and asked what was up. I told him, and he handed me thirty bucks to go buy a fishing pole.

All right, God.

So I got into this prayer thing. The first thing I prayed about was what to do when the summer was over. I didn't want to go back to my hometown, because that was not an option, I knew myself well enough to know what would happen if I went back into that situation.

Then the lady at the post office started telling me about this place called Joshua. She said, "You should go to this place. It's a discipleship program. You go there and study the Bible. You can't listen to music. You can't watch movies. You can't date. You separate yourself from the world—for nine months."

So I said, "You got any other ideas?"

People kept talking to me about this place, and I lied to them. I said, "I would *love* to go to Joshua, but I can't afford it. It costs $8,000.00, and *unfortunately* for me, I just don't have that kind of money."

Then my mother called and said, "I heard you want to go to Joshua. I'll pay for it if you want to go."

How did my mother find out about Joshua? I hadn't talked to her in weeks! "Mom, who told you about Joshua? And who told you I wanted to go there? I certainly don't want to go there! I can't listen to music. I can't date. Does that sound like something I would want to do? —And besides, I think it's filled up."

My mom kept insisting that I go and ask if there were any openings, so finally I told her I would—just to get her off my back, but I had no intentions of actually going.

Then this thing started bugging me, and it wouldn't stop! So I went and talked to the director. "I know you have a waiting list of like a hundred people... but my mother's offered to pay for me... so I just want to let you know... because I keep feeling this *thing* telling me to do stuff... and I've got to tell you, so it'll quit bugging me."

The director's wife said, "Didn't a spot open up today?"

I said, "No it didn't."

The director told me he'd check into it and get back to me. Two days later he told me I'd been accepted! I remember laughing because I knew it was God. I still didn't want to go, but I was excited because I knew I was finally doing God's will—and if it was God's will, then how could it be wrong?

I spent nine months without music or TV, I spent nine months studying the Bible, and I spent nine months finding out that Jesus really *is* the Great I Am! The God who made the universe, the One who said, "Let there be light," and there was light, humbled himself and came into the world as a man. Our Maker, who is so big and so powerful and so sovereign, loved us so much that he allowed himself to be tortured and hung on a cross in order to save us from our sin, and from hell. He did all this for *us!* Not because he had to, but because he *wanted* to, because he *loves* us! The moment this really sunk in, I started crying.

> **"In the beginning was the Word,**
> **and the Word was with God, and the**
> **Word was God. All things were made by him,**
> **and without him was not any thing made...**
> **And the Word was made flesh**
> **and dwelt among us..."**
> (John 1:1, 3, 14 KJV)

When my time at Joshua was coming to an end, I began praying about what to do next. From the first month at the program, people had been telling me that God was going to use me to counsel drug addicts. I loved this idea, and I prayed that God would make it so—but then I learned about an internship at a church—in *Hawaii! Yes! Thank You, Lord!*

But God had something different in mind.

Ken Graves came to speak at Joshua. He told me I should come to the School of Ministry at his church—in *Maine!* He told me, "It's going to be really hard. You're not going to get a lot of sleep. You're not going to get a lot of time off. You're either going to be working, going to school, studying, preaching, or sleeping."

So I said, "You got any other ideas?" I was NOT going to MAINE!

Then that thing started *bugging* me again.

Here in Maine, one of the things I'm doing is counseling drug addicts at the church's residential discipleship program. I get to hang out and love on the guys who are recovering from addictions, and I get to relate to them what I've learned. Some of them don't want to be here, but the guys who genuinely devote themselves to the Lord... well, seeing them grow is just so cool!

I now understand that that thing bugging me is God's Spirit. I know how much he loves me and I know he wants to give me the desires of my heart. (Psalm 37:4) When I was at Joshua, I started praying about getting back into wrestling. I love wrestling, and it's always been my dream to be a wrestling coach.

Just last week, Ken said, "You know, they might need help with the wrestling team..."

God is good.
He really is.
If you've got the Holy Spirit bugging you.
Just do it.
There's no point in arguing.
He's always right.
Trust him.
God is good.
He really is.

The best thing I've been able to accomplish with my own hands is almost killing myself. The best decisions I ever made got me into the worst places. How God can use someone like me, I still don't know. But he can. He is fully capable of running people's lives.

> *"For I know the plans*
> *I have for you," declares the LORD,*
> *"plans to prosper you and not to harm you,*
> *plans to give you hope and a future. Then you*
> *will call upon me and come and pray to me,*
> *and I will listen to you. You will seek me*
> *and find me when you seek me*
> *with all your heart."*
> (Jeremiah 29:11-13 NIV)

Give him your life. You won't be sorry.

To learn more about Hume Lake or Joshua,
log onto www.Humelake.org.

To learn more about the CC Central Maine
School of Ministry:
go to www.ccbangor.org
or call Calvary Chapel at (207) 991-9555

From Dealer to Healer
Chuck's Story

I got saved when I was sixteen,
but knowing the Lord, and walking with him
are two very different things.

It started with cigarettes when I was nine years old, and marijuana soon after that. Before I joined the Marine Corps, drugs were taking control of my life, then after I joined, I became thoroughly enslaved. In the military I fell in with a bunch of hard core users, and started shooting up. The quantity we did was unbelievable, we heard of men dying from smaller amounts than what we were doing.

So it wasn't long before I went AWOL (absent without leave), and I didn't plan on going back. But then I recommitted my life to the Lord and turned myself in. That's when I found out that even if you crawl back and apologize, they still throw you in the brig.

Back with my buddies, I started using again, and soon went AWOL again. This time I somehow ended up at a Bible study in Costa Mesa, California, where, after the service, I went forward to talk to Pastor Chuck Smith about the Marines, and about the drugs, hoping that he would say, "*Oh yeah, you need to stay away from there you know.*" But instead he brought me over to his assistant pastor, who just *happened* to be a retired Marine Drill Instructor, who just *happen* to be some of the meanest guys in the Marine Corps! I braced myself for a severe chastening, but instead he was very nice. He laid out scriptural reasons for why I needed to go back and serve my country.

So I went back, again, and got thrown in the brig,

again. This pattern repeated itself several times: Go AWOL, recommit to Jesus, turn myself in, get thrown in the brig, start using again... In a little over two years in the military, I spent ten months AWOL, ten months in prison, and six months good time. Eventually the Marines got fed up with me and set me free.

But I was still in bondage.

Back home in Oregon, I hooked up with a couple of friends and spent the next five years as a weekend junkie. We'd work all week then get high all weekend. But the money we made working wasn't enough, so we started stealing. Canoes disappeared from the roofs of cars, lawnmowers vanished from front yards, trucks found themselves without radiators, and the telephone company was losing copper wire left and right... We made over a thousand dollars a week selling stolen goods, and it's a miracle we were never caught.

But then my sister asked if I wanted to move to Southern California with her. She and her husband had been praying for a long time, and they thought if they could get me away from my friends, maybe I'd stop using, and they were right.

I partied all the way down on the train, but the minute my feet hit the pavement, I felt the Lord telling me, *The party's over.* From that moment, my drug use came to a screeching halt, my gutter street language disappeared, and my life changed completely. I was thrown in with a bunch of Christians, and, for *ten years,* my life was Christ centered. I was completely free from the bondage of drugs and alcohol.

Until one night when my uncle handed me a joint.

> ***"Stand fast therefore in the liberty with which Christ has made us free, and do not again be held with the yoke of bondage."***
> (Galatians 5:1 MKJV)

As time went on, Chuck married a woman he met at church. But the marriage ended after three and a half years when she found out he was stealing from their house fund to buy pot. Soon after this, he married another woman he'd met at church. He told his second wife about the marijuana, but she had no idea the extent of it. He was smoking at least three or four joints a day. They had two boys and were together for several years before Chuck went back to work, and the problems escalated.

For three years my wife worked, and I was Mr. Mom. I took good care of my boys, but I was still sneaking joints every chance I got. (There was never a shortage of Visine or cologne at our house.) For awhile I got away with this—but then I went back to work.

I was working graveyard when I first snorted a small amount of crystal meth to help me stay awake. And I did stay awake, for *two days!* It wasn't long before I was snorting all the time, but I lied to myself. I told myself, if I wasn't shooting, I wasn't using. This was a lie from the pit of hell.

My wife didn't have a clue what I was doing, but she knew something was up because I went from a hefty one hundred ninety pounds to a skinny one-fifty in six months. Then I started fighting with her all the time, and one night I hauled off and hit her. So she got on the phone and had me hauled off to jail.

When I got out, I begged and pleaded and promised that I would never ever hit her again if she took me back. But I didn't keep my promise, and I found myself in jail, again. This time she didn't let me come home for two months, and when I went back home, I only managed to stay clean for two weeks.

Before she kicked me out, I lost my job. After she kicked me out, she handed me divorce papers. So I found myself with no job, no family, and no place to live. Somehow I managed to find a job and a room in a little share-the-bathroom-down-the-hall transient hotel. I wanted to clean myself up, so I started going to a secular rehab program and I gave up speed. But after testing positive for pot, I never went back. Then I found out the guy down the hall was a speed dealer.

So much for giving up speed.

For the next year, a third of my pay went for rent, a third went for my kids, and the other third went for my habit. But after awhile, I felt if I didn't get away from there, I would die.

So I came up with a brilliant plan. I got all my stuff together and set out to go back-packing until I ran out of money. I brought my drug dealer along, he brought an eight ball of speed, and we set out to climb Mt. Whitney, the tallest mountain in the United States. It's a six hour climb to the top, but it took us four days! We'd sleep till noon, do a couple of lines, walk for an hour or two, then set up camp and do more lines. When we finally got to the top, we were low on food and out of speed. We had two options: We could either ration our food and hike twenty miles a day for the next two days, or, we could turn around and go right back out. We hiked out in six and a half hours what took us four days to get in.

At this point, I decided to hitchhike up to Oregon to see if one of my brothers or sisters would take me in, but no one would have anything to do with me. I was nothing more than an emaciated human being, a stick rail of a person with sunken cheeks. No one was going to trust me, especially with their kids around. Every door was closed. So I hitchhiked back to Southern California, and a guy I used to work with let me sleep on his couch for a couple of weeks. But then he found out I was back on drugs, and I found myself back on the street.

So I called my wife and told her I was leaving the state. She wanted to know where I was going, and I told her I was just going to hitchhike until I found something. It was New Year's weekend, 1996. I hitchhiked down to Long Beach where I met up with my nephew and his wife. We partied all weekend, then I called my wife again.

She'd been doing some research and told me about a place called U-Turn 4 Christ. She said, "They'll take you. They're a drug and alcohol place, and they're right over in Perris." I didn't want to listen to her. But she kept saying. "They *will* take you. I've already talked to them." And the more she talked, the more I realized—I had no other options.

My nephew dropped me off at the train station. I took the train, then a bus, then had to walk a few miles overland. I smoked my last joint as I walked up to the place, and as I walked through the gate, I prayed, *"Lord if they accept me, I'm back for good."*

Sure enough, they took me in.

I thought I had to clean myself up before the Lord would take me back, but I was wrong. In his infinite grace, he took a wretched, drug-addicted, wife-beating loser like me, and *he* did the cleaning. He took what the world had rejected and turned me into a respectable human being. And because of his Grace, my life is now committed to serving him and serving others who find themselves in bondage to drugs and alcohol.

> ***"Therefore if the Son shall make you free, you shall be free indeed."***
> (John 8:36 MKJV)

When I entered U-Turn, I'd known Jesus for thirty-five years, but knowing him and walking with him are two *very* different things. I always knew he existed. I could see him in nature, and I accepted his presence. I acknowledged him like my shadow, but I was doing what *I* wanted to do. Walking with the Lord means to follow his ways, to do his will, and to obey his Word. And when you do this, you are free indeed. I started walking with the Lord on January 2, 1996, and I don't regret a single step.

> ***"As you therefore have received Christ Jesus the Lord, so walk in him."***
> (Colossians 2:6 MKJV)

> ***"Blessed are the undefiled in the way, who walk in the law of the LORD."***
> (Psalm 119:1 KJV)

Some time before I went to U-Turn, my sister told my brother she'd given up and stopped praying for me. My little brother laid into her and said, "How *dare* you think my God can't help him! He's our brother, and God can do *anything.* You need to be praying for him!" He convicted her, and she started praying again. The day I walked into U-Turn was my sister's birthday. God heard those prayers, and he brought me to U-Turn. Don't ever give up on a family member, or anybody else. Just pray for them. Prayer *will* change things.

On average, the success rate for men who complete the U-Turn program is well above 50%, which is far higher than secular rehab programs that don't focus on God's Word. **To learn more about U-Turn 4 Christ, visit their web site at www.uturn4christ.com**

In his infinite patience, the Lord
freed Chuck. But amazingly, this wouldn't
be the last time God saved his neck.

In 2001 I came to Maine from California to open up another U-Turn. The first night I was at Calvary Chapel, the pastor introduced me to the congregation and explained what I was there to do. After the service a man came up and welcomed me. He was a doctor, and he told me to let him know if there was anything he could do for me.
Then one night I saw him in church and asked if he'd take a look at the mole on my temple. He looked at it, but was more interested in looking at the lump on my neck. It was about an inch around and stuck out about an inch. He told me I should have it checked. But since I didn't have any money, or insurance, I decided not to worry about it,

and I put it out of my mind.

But the doctor didn't forget. He was in a weekly Bible study with a group of surgeons, and he told them about my situation. One of the surgeons told him to send me in, and that he wouldn't charge me for the visit. So I went in, and the doctor took a needle biopsy, but I didn't understand what had happened. When I left the hospital with a bandage on my neck, I thought the lump was gone.

But it wasn't gone, and a few days later I was called in to discuss the results of the biopsy. I was having a hard time understanding the doctor because he was using a lot of medical terms. He was saying the lump was malignant, and that it had metastasized into my neck, and that I was lucky it hadn't gone into my lymph nodes. I didn't have a clue what he was talking about, so finally I said, "Should I be concerned about all of this?"

He chuckled and sort of patted me on the shoulder, and said, "Yeah. This is the Big One." He told me I had cancer, and that metastasized meant that it had started somewhere else. He didn't like the look of my tonsils so he was going to look at them the following week. I was a little choked up, but I thought I could tough it out, and I *wasn't* going to cry about it.

When I went back to the church, Sheila, the secretary, looked at me, and said, "Well?" When I said, "Its cancer," she started crying, then I started crying, and then Pastor Ken came in. When he found out what all the crying was about, he said, "You take my office and make all the phone calls you need."

So I got through the rest of that day, calling my family and friends, telling them I had cancer.

The following week I went in for a tonsillectomy. They put me under and took out my right tonsil. The doctor said, "We got it all." So once again, I was under the impression that the problem had been taken care of. I thought the cancer was gone, but as it turned out, he had gotten all the *original* cancer in the tonsil, but the metastasized cancer was still in my neck—so they scheduled me for radiation.

Radiation is a weird thing. I was strapped down to a bed with a machine going over me, but *nothing* was happening. I could see nothing. I could feel nothing, but little by little, over time, my energy was completely drained, and large ulcers began forming on the sides of my tongue. Eating became excruciatingly painful, and I could barely taste anything. Ken and I would go out for lunch, but I couldn't eat, nothing tasted good. I would take one bite, then Ken would get to eat the rest. I was devastated!

Because I couldn't eat, I had to drink Ensure, and that stuff was just *gagging* me! I forced myself to drink one or two cans a day, but I still lost thirty pounds in a month. Then the doctor threatened to put me on IVs if I didn't maintain my weight, so I had to drink at least six cans of this disgusting stuff every day. And you know what, the radiation didn't kill all of my taste buds, the ones that could taste Ensure were still alive!

After about a month of radiation, the nurse asked if I was ready for pain medication. Because I used to be a heroin addict, a speed freak, a pot smoker, *and* a drunk, I kept putting it off. But then one day the doctor wrote a prescription for pain meds, and I gave in. He put me on Oxycontin, a manmade heroin. I had to take a five milligram tablet every couple of hours, but as the weeks went by the doctor said I could take two, then three.

The meds worked great for the pain, but there were side effects. My stomach was always upset, and I could barely keep my eyes open. I was afraid to sit in church because I thought at any minute I would nod off and snore, or worse, fall out of my chair. I got to the point where I was so tired, I would fall asleep at red lights. The drug was messing up my mind, and I didn't recognize the danger I was putting myself in. One day while driving, I had the guys from U-Turn behind me, and it crossed my mind that if I started to go off the road, they would honk and wake me up!

Another time I was giving the assistant pastor's daughter a ride home. I swear I did *not* nod off, but she told her dad that I did, and when Pastor Ken heard about it, he said, "That's it, you're moving in with me and Jeanette, and I'm going to be your driver from now on." So I moved in with Ken.

Because of the nausea and the Ensure, I felt sick all the time. Ken has a Dodge pickup truck with a passenger handle on the windshield frame. We'd be driving along, and without saying anything, I'd hang onto the handle, open the door, and heave out the side of the truck. Ken would be yelling, "Let me pull over! Let me pull over!" To this day Ken says he never knew what those handles were for, until he had me in the truck.

And so it went on for about another month: living at Ken's, getting radiation, doing the Oxycontin, drinking the Ensure, and hanging from the truck handle.

When the radiation therapy ended after two months, I went in for a check-up. Again I hoped the cancer was gone, but the doctor said I needed a *radical neck dissection!* They were going to cut away the whole right side of my neck from front to back! Radiation had failed. The lump was still there. You could see it. You could feel it. You could practically hang a hat on it!

I asked the doctor how long it would be before I could travel to see my kids. He said, "See them before the operation because if they see you after, it'll be too radical for them."

So he scheduled the operation, I had another MRI, and the next day I boarded a plane for California.

The doctor said, it would be at *least* six months before my taste buds came back, but amazingly, two weeks later, I was taking my kids out to restaurants and eating a whole meal—but I still wouldn't eat ice cream. Before the radiation I would eat about a half a gallon of ice cream every night, but after, it just wasn't the same. Someone asked me why, and I said, "You know how ice cream dances on your tongue? —Well, it quit dancing." It was seven months before I started eating ice cream again.

After three weeks in California, I went back to Maine and found a message on my machine from the doctor's office. They wanted me to come in right away. So I called. The secretary said, "The doctor needs to talk to you. How soon can you get here?"

Whatever God wanted to do was okay with me. I figured if he wanted to take me home, he'd take me home. If he wanted to use me with half a neck, he'd use me with half a neck. Actually, I was excited about the possibility of going home to be with the Lord, I'd never once prayed for healing, but the way the secretary told me to come right away had me worried. I thought maybe the MRI showed something worse, maybe the cancer had spread.

When I got to the office, I asked, "*What's up?* Is it good news or bad news?"

The nurse was smiling, and she said, "When the doctor came back from his vacation, he couldn't understand why he had you scheduled for surgery."

Just then the doctor came in and started feeling around on my neck. He asked if I could feel the lump. I said, "No, I thought I'd misplaced it!" In California I was trying to tell people about this lump, but I couldn't find it! Then the doctor told me that the last MRI showed *no trace* of the cancer. All it detected was some scar tissue from the radiation. That was all! They were stumped by it.

The lump was still there when I'd finished radiation treatments, but now it was completely gone! I said, "Well praise God! You wouldn't believe how many people have been praying for me!"

It was true. *I* hadn't prayed for healing, but I had friends and family all over the world praying for me: friends in Maine, South Carolina, Tennessee; family in California, Oregon, and Florida; and friends in India, Europe, and the Philippines... They were all praying, and God answered their prayers. The cancer was gone! And *this* time when the doctor said it was gone, I wasn't misunderstanding him, it was *gone!* There wasn't a trace to be found.

"...pray for one another, that you may be healed. The effectual fervent prayer of a righteous one avails much."
(James 5:16 MKJV)

And not only did the cancer disappear, the medical bills vanished right along with it. My doctor sent me his bill just so I could see it. It was thirty *thousand* dollars. St. Joe's hospital wrote off twenty or thirty thousand, and Eastern Maine Medical Center wrote off about the same.

My medical bills were close to a hundred thousand dollars, but I never had to paid a single penny.

*Five years after his ordeal
with cancer, Pastor Chuck is cancer free,
clean and sober, and still walking with the Lord.*

And the ice cream just keeps on dancing.

Pastor Chuck says,

"Praise God!"

The Appointment
Kim's Story

I wanted to cancel the appointment; there was simply too much going on. There were only five shopping days left until Christmas, and I was *working* three of those days. Besides, the kids didn't really *need* their hair cut, and Debbie wouldn't mind if I rescheduled. I knew she wouldn't. —I *really* wanted to cancel that appointment.

But I didn't.

I told Garrett and Jillian on the way to the salon that they were *not* going to stay to play with Samantha when we were done. We were going to go in, get their hair cuts done, and get out of there! Period.

When we arrived at Kid Kutters, the place was a madhouse. There were three other moms in the waiting area, and a total of nine kids (including mine) now playing loudly together all over the shop. To my relief, Debbie was able to take Jillian right away, and soon Garrett was in the chair having his turn. When he was done, I was ready to go.

But the kids begged, "Just five minutes, Mommy? *Please?* We never get to play with Samantha! She's going to put in a movie. Please, Mommy? *Pleeeeease?*"

I looked over at Debbie's little seven-year-old Samantha, a beautiful dark haired girl, and such a sweetheart. She was helping kids get arranged around the little TV set and handing out Christmas candies from a dish.

"Oh all *right*. But only *five minutes!*" Little did I know they would be five of the most important minutes of my life! I walked over to the coat rack and got my kids' coats and boots ready so we could hurry right out. Then I heard Debbie's voice. She was *panicked!*

"Oh my GOD! Somebody help me! She's CHOKING! Somebody help! Somebody HELP SAMANTHA!"

I looked over and saw Samantha clutching at her mother with a look of horror painted on her face, and she was turning bright red. Now normally I'm kind of a nervous person, a real worrier, but as I looked over at them, a perfect peace came over me. It was a feeling of perfect protection and calm, as though someone else had taken control. I parted the crowd and pointed at one of the other moms. "Call 911. She isn't breathing!" I squatted down in front of Samantha. "I'm going to help you."

Debbie had collapsed in her chair and was turning green with panic.

I turned Samantha around, put my arms around her, and began to perform the Heimlich maneuver. I did it once, twice, three times. After the fourth, Samantha suddenly took in a deep breath. I asked her, "Is it still in there?" She nodded yes, so I continued with the upward thrusts to her sternum. One—two—three. With this last one, a red and white peppermint candy shot out of her mouth and landed five feet away in the corner, and she collapsed in my arms. I asked her, "Are you okay, honey?" She nodded yes, so I picked her up, and put her in her mother's lap. At this point, I think everyone in the shop was crying.

After my kids came over and hugged Samantha, and after everything was said and done, I had time to help my kids with coats and boots, get them out to the car, get them strapped into their car seats, and was ready to pull out—when the paramedics arrived. By that time it would have been too late to save Samantha.

I really wanted to cancel that appointment—but I didn't. I felt compelled to keep it.

> *"I thank him who has*
> *given me strength, Christ Jesus*
> *our Lord, because he judged*
> *me faithful, appointing me*
> *to his service,"*
> (1 Timothy 1:12 ESV)

Words from a thankful Mom:

I pray all the time for the Lord to protect my children, and I believe the Lord brought Kim here that day to save Samantha. She was the only one in the shop who knew the Heimlich maneuver. If she hadn't been there, Samantha wouldn't be here.
It was a miracle.
And this incident changed me. I've always appreciated my daughter, she's a gift, but now my time with Samantha is even more precious. I take nothing for granted.
I love my job; I wouldn't be working with children if I didn't. But now every time a child comes into my shop I'm that much more aware of how very precious they are.

The day after Kim performed the Heimlich maneuver on Samantha, Debbie called the Red Cross to see about getting signed up for CPR classes. She told them what Kim had done, and they suggested she nominate Kim for the annual Hero's Award. Several months later Debbie received a call. Kim had won!

I was so happy to get that call from the Red Cross! I'm just so **HAPPY** that she **WON!** *Because she saved my baby!*

Salt and Light
Elizabeth's Story

E-liz-a-beth (i liz' e beth), consecrated to God.
con-se-crate (kon' se krat'), *v.*, 1. to make or declare sacred; set apart or dedicate to the service of God.

(Elizabeth speaks in imperfect English with a Spanish accent.)
As a young girl in El Salvador, I live in a Christian home, but I never believe in God one hundred percent.
Until this happen.
I was, nineteen, married, pregnant—I was thinking, God is not today, God is tomorrow.
I put myself before God.
We go to church a few times. But I don't really believe. Then one time the pastor ask us, will we have a Bible study in our home? So we say okay.
There was, many people in my house. Everybody is ready. We already pray. Everybody is waiting for me because I am busy cooking, making snacks, and a type of drink in a pressure cooker. It's made with corn meal and sugar inside a coffee can. The can heats inside a pot, and it builds up pressure. A *lot* of pressure.
So the people wait, and I go into the bathroom to look at myself in the mirror. I am thinking, "Oh I am so beautiful. I am *very* beautiful!"
I loved myself before God.
So I took my time.
I come back, and I say, "Okay. I'm ready." —And I'm not thinking about what I'm doing—because I'm thinking about *me*.

> *"Pride goes before*
> *destruction, and a haughty*
> *spirit before a fall."*
> (Proverbs 16:18 MKJV)

I open the pressure cooker, and the drink explode in my face.

In my country the hospital is far away. They want to take me, but I say no because I'm pregnant; they will put me on antibiotics, and it will harm the baby I think. So I refuse that.

That night I don't sleep. My face is burning, burning, *burning* HOT.

The next day a relative of my husband come and they take me to a witch. *A witch!* I try to block this out; it was *so ridiculous!* She speak in a strange language, and she give to us some cream, *voo doo* cream.

My face become—very infected.

Someone else give to me some cream from the pharmacy. My face get worse. Full of puss. Dripping. I was very sick. Very sick and very depressed. So depressed—I don't care anymore.

I feel dead.

On the third day I look like a monster. A black monster. Charcoal on my face. Very scary. Very scary and very dangerous. I look in the mirror, and I say, "I guess I'm not beautiful anymore."

My husband look at me, and he say, "You know you will need plastic surgery."

The fourth day the pastor come to my house. "You need to go to the hospital," he say.

"No. I'm not going to the hospital."

"Do you mind if I pray for you?" he ask me.

"Yeah. You can pray for me."

So he pray. He say, "I pray, God, you will give me some miracle that I can bring for this girl's face." He say I need to have faith. And I did. I was feeling confident.

Then he went home. The next day he come back, and he say, "You know I pray, and God lead me to look in a book, and it open to just the right page! It say to wash your face with salt and water, and your skin will heal."

Salt water! You know how painful is that?

But I say, "Well... If you pray about it, God have a purpose for it. Let's do that."

Before he wash my face we pray again. He pray for healing, but in my heart, I pray for forgiveness. I say, "I know God that this is your day. I know you have called me to serve you. I give everything to you. Forgive me. I'm yours." And I feel *light!* So light! And so happy! I never feel so happy in all my life! And the happiness last, for—*years!*

> *"Give joy to the soul of Your servant...For You, Lord, are good and ready to forgive, and rich in mercy to all those who call on You."*
> (Psalm 86:4-5 MKJV)

Then he put the cloth on my face. It was so *refreshing!* Cooling. Like when you are very thirsty, and you drink a BIG glass of water. Aaaaahhhhh! *So* relaxing! *Wonderful!* I want more and more...

Every day for three days he come to my house, and he wash my face with salt water. On the third day, my face start to be dry, so we leave it alone.

Four days after this my face is completely dry.

A month pass, and my face was ugly. I had to walk with a veil over my face because people couldn't help looking at me. But now I don't care, I don't feel shame. I feel content, and I don't care what I look like. I have God, and he fill me with joy!

I don't put myself before God anymore.

After awhile I have my baby, and my face is normal again. Yes!

God is so good.

God is SO *good!*

He bring to me the pastor, so I can have salt water to save my face, but *far* better, he bring to me Jesus, so I can have the *living water* to save *me.*

*"Jesus answered,
...the water that I shall give him shall be in him a well of water springing up into everlasting life."*
(John 4:13-14 MKJV)

"...everyone who shall call upon the name of the Lord shall be saved."
(Acts 2:21 MKJV)

Words from Elizabeth

Always love God more than people,
because no matter how much they love you,
they will always let you down.
God will never let you down.

It's very simple.
You just need to open your eyes and say,
"Oh. That's right. You're God!"
You've been there all my life!

He's so wonderful.

Knowing God.
It's like having huge piles of gold
that keeps piling and piling...
and you just want to give it away!
'Cause there's no place to put it!

Heaven
Lily's Story

Five year old Lily was afraid to go to heaven because she didn't know what it would be like.

Two years before, at the age of three, the little girl had been diagnosed with cancer throughout her body and had undergone two surgeries to remove a large tumor from her abdomen. And after this, she'd faced two *years* of chemotherapy—but the cancer was still spreading.

So the hospital staff told the family, all they could do now, was make her comfortable.

"He's fishing! He's fishing in heaven!" Lily told her nurse one day when she entered the room.

"What are you talking about, Lily?" the nurse asked.

"The boy next door! He's happy now! He's fishing in heaven!"

There was no way Lily could have known the boy in the next room had died. There was a picture in his room of him propped up holding a fishing pole—but Lily had never been in his room.

Perhaps this was God's way of easing Lily's fears about heaven.

The little girl continued to get worse, and then one day, when her mother was with her, Lily started counting. Gazing up into the corner of her hospital room, she counted, "One, two, three..." She got as far as ten and then started over, because that was as high as she could count.

She did this several times.

Finally her mother asked, "What are you doing, Lily?"

Lily answered, "I'm counting the angels, Mommy."

The very next day Lily found out for herself what heaven is like.

***"And God shall wipe away
all tears from their eyes; and there
shall be no more death, neither sorrow,
nor crying, neither shall there be any
more pain: for the former things
are passed away."***
(Revelation 21:4 KJV)

The nurse who shared this story said she's heard of at least three other children, under the age of six, who saw angels a day or two before they died.

Tracy's Song
Joanie's Story

Matthew didn't know how Tracy had died.
That's what made the song so amazing.

A phone call came into the Hampden Police Department early that Wednesday morning in November of 2002. An abandoned car had been found on a tiny dirt road way up behind Green Lake. The police had been looking for the car, and its owner, since the Friday before. Was there any hope the young mother would be found alive?

Tracy was my cousin, but to me she was more like a sister. She was dark and pretty, with long, beautiful eyelashes, and a gentle way about her. When we were very little everyone called us "*kissing* cousins" because that's how we greeted one another. And as we grew, we shared time and secrets, laughter and heart aches. We stayed up late every chance we got, talking and giggling, until inevitably she would fall asleep on me while I was still talking.

Tracy was my favorite cousin, and my best friend.

But when we reached our teen years, her life was thrown into turmoil, and our friendship began to suffer. Both of her parents passed away, and she began to cling more and more to her boyfriend. We kept in touch, but there was a wall between us, and she no longer opened up to me.

As an adult, Tracy appeared to have her life together. She was smart and creative, and she loved the out-of-doors almost as much as she adored her two boys. As a successful accountant for the hospital, she always bought the best, and didn't seem to have a want in the world. But all that glitters is not gold.

Tracy had endured the most painful year of her life before disappearing. Crushed under the weight of a failed marriage, she desperately reached out to anyone and everyone. She hadn't had a decent night's sleep in months, and was almost always on the verge of tears. In an effort to stay healthy for her sons, she forced herself to eat, but grew thinner by the day, and counseling and antidepressants did little to lift the weight of hopelessness. I will never forget the words she whispered to me over the phone one night.

"I want my mother."

Her mother had been gone for seventeen years.

Everywhere she turned there seemed to be conflicting advice. Some told her to believe in herself. Others told her to trust in God. She attended church with me a few times, but mostly just stared blankly, or cried. She told me she had been listening to K-Lov (a Christian radio station) and that she had tried to "give it over to Jesus," but that it hadn't helped. She didn't *feel* any better for doing so.

But *I* began to notice changes in her. She said she'd been praying that God would help her to be strong, and then had felt renewed strength at those moments when she most needed it.

It seemed like her heart was being changed. She was doing better emotionally, smiling more and crying less, and I started to believe that she would pull through and be okay. I began to see glimpses of the Tracy I had known as a child—my favorite cousin and my best friend.

But then shortly after experiencing a crisis, she became unemotional. She appeared almost numb, somehow resolute. Then she simply disappeared, leaving a host of family and friends frantically searching.

The search team quickly assembled at the site of the abandoned car, and hours later, a hound picked up her scent. She was found on a little hill deep in the forest. Apparently she had become tired and had sat down under a tree to rest.

An empty bottle of sleeping pills was found in the car.

Friends and family came from all over the country to attend Tracy's funeral. The pastor spoke comforting words to a crowded room, and gave a presentation of the Bible as a guide for life. Smiling images of a beautiful Tracy rolled by on a TV screen. People shared songs and stories—and tried to understand.

A few days later my husband was compiling a CD of songs from the funeral to send to Tracy's siblings, when for the first time, we realized that one of the songs not only mirrored Tracy's state of mind in the months before she died, but it also described Tracy's death. It had been sung by the pastor's son, Matthew, and it contained words which could have come directly from Tracy in her last moments of life. I was curious to know how Matthew had found a song which so perfectly described the situation. But when we asked him, he was amazed to learn how the song mirrored Tracy's death, he hadn't known how she had died. He'd felt strongly that God wanted him to sing that particular song, but he'd had no idea why.

The song is by The David Crowder Band and is called *All That I Can Say.*

Tracy was walking through the woods, alone, after taking a bottle of sleeping pills, when the drugs began to take effect.

The song begins, *"Lord I'm tired, so tired from walking, and Lord I'm so alone. And Lord the dark is creeping in, is creeping up, to swallow me. I think I'll stop and rest here awhile. —This is all that I can say right now. This is all that I can give. That's my everything.*

She must have been calling out to God as she sat under the tree and began to fade from consciousness. The song goes on, *"Oh and did you see me crying? And did you hear me call your name? Wasn't it you I gave my heart to? I wish you'd remember where you set it down."*

The Bible tells us that God will never leave us or forsake us. As she released her final breath, I believe that Tracy suddenly became aware that she was *not* alone. The song's last stanza says, *"I didn't notice you were standing here. I didn't know that that was you holding me. I didn't notice you were crying too. I didn't know that that was you washing my feet."*

It was raining on that cold November day, and as Tracy sat huddled under the tree, her eyes were opened, and she suddenly became aware that the drops of water falling upon her feet—were the very tears of God.

> **"... because God has said, 'Never will I leave you; never will I forsake you.'"**
> (Hebrews 13:5 NIV)

> **"The Lord is close to the brokenhearted and saves those who are crushed in spirit."**
> (Psalm 34:18 NIV)

My Shield
Daniel's Story

***"The LORD is
my strength and my shield;
my heart trusted in him,
and I am helped..."***
(Psalm 28:7 KJV)

    I was riding on the top of the vehicle when the bomb went off. A roadside IED. I thought for sure I was going to die.
    But I didn't.
    It was as though there was an invisible shield all around me. The debris was flying at my face, and I was knocked unconscious, but nothing hit me—nothing but a tiny piece of shrapnel that just clipped the end of my nose.
    Some of the other guys were killed.
    I know without a doubt that God protected me.

***"Keep me, O LORD,
from the hands of the wicked;
preserve me from the violent man..."***
(Psalm 140:4 KJV)

Daniel was twenty-three years old and serving as a United States Army medic on his third tour in Iraq when the roadside bomb exploded underneath his vehicle.

After this, all of my buddies kept asking me, "Why are you always so calm? Why aren't you afraid?" I told them, "Because I truly trust in the Lord."

"God says, 'I will save those who love me and will protect those who acknowledge me as LORD.'"
(Psalm 91:14 GNB)

Losing Matthew
Barbara's Story

I lost my son when he was eight years old. No, he didn't die—but a part of me died that day.

He was a gift from God, my little Matthew. I didn't think I could get pregnant because I had tried for a year and a half with no success. But finally when I called out to God, he answered my prayer, and it was only *after* we named him, that we found out, Matthew means *a gift from God.*

And he was.

We had a wonderful relationship, Matthew and I. For four and a half years, I was his adoring mother, and he was My Little Bugaboo. He used to *love* the Tickle-Bug Song: *"There's a tickle-bug, and he's on the loose, in Matthew's room, in Matthew's room...."* Then I would tickle him like crazy, and he would laugh his head off. I often took him to the park to play, and we went to church every Sunday—but we *had* to bring all of our friends along. Matthew called them the Bumble Critters. There was Bumble Bad, Bumble Good, Bumble Bug, and Bumble Bed. *I* couldn't see them, but Matthew could—and we couldn't go *anywhere* without them. He was the cutest kid in the whole world, my little Matthew.

One time I had to pull the car off the road because I was very upset over something. Matthew unhooked himself, climbed over the seat, and wrapped his little arms around me until I stopped crying. He was only eighteen months old. He was a very compassionate little guy, my Little Bugaboo.

But somehow, over time, things changed. Matthew's father and I split up, and I moved to another apartment to be closer to my mom. We moved away from all that was familiar. I was away from my new friends, I was away from my support network, and I stopped going to church. Then I met up with some friends from high school. They offered me a drink. At first I said no. But after awhile I caved, and it was all downhill from there.

> **"Do not get drunk with wine, which will only ruin you; instead be filled with the Spirit."**
> (Ephesians 5:18)

A year went by, and we were evicted from our apartment and were forced to live out of my car for awhile. That is until I met another guy, and Matthew and I moved in with him. As time went on this new boyfriend and I drank more and more, and I started doing drugs. At best Matthew was being ignored, and at worst he was being exposed to some very erratic behavior. If he was bad, I spanked him. So with all that was going on, it's no mystery why he started acting up in school.

More and more, he got into trouble. More and more, I spanked him. Then when I promised to go on a field trip with his class but was unable to keep that promise, his behavior went from bad to worse. Every single day Matthew was getting into trouble, mouthing off, throwing pencils, *spitting* on people. Every single day I spanked him—until one day, I spanked him so hard, he wasn't able to sit down. That was the day the babysitter reported me. That was the day I lost my son.

At first I was *furious* with everyone, and I drank even more. At first I refused to take the blame, and I took more drugs. I was hurt, I was angry, and I was doing everything I could to block out my life. But after awhile, I started to realize, I didn't want to live without my boy.

So the day my boyfriend locked me *in* the house (he nailed all the doors shut thinking I had gone out) was the day I stopped drinking. I climbed out through a window, and had my mother drive me to Acadia Hospital where I had myself admitted for detox.

After being sober for only two days, a meeting was set up between me and Matthew's psychiatrist. I thought he was going to help me be a better mother. I thought he was going to help me see my son again. But I was wrong. He walked in and made sure I *knew* what a horrible, horrible, *HORRIBLE* mother I had been. And then he left.

Soon after this I was convicted of assaulting my son and put on probation for a year. I immediately went about the process of being able to have supervised visits. I did everything the State required: I obtained a psychiatric evaluation, I started paying child support, and I stayed clean and sober.

I was still angry at the psychiatrist, but the more I thought about it, the more I realized—he was right. With a clearer mind, I could see just how badly I had treated my son. Then over time, I started to feel just a little bit grateful. Somewhere in my heart I began to believe that they had done the right thing by taking him away. So now that I believed I was the most horrible mother that ever existed, the visits were scheduled to start.

I hadn't seen Matthew at all during the three months he had been living with his father and step-mother, and I was very nervous about our first visit. I don't think I slept more than a few hours the night before, but I needn't have worried. Matthew and I had a blast! We played games together, I read to him, we had all kinds of fun!

For two precious hours, two times a week, I was able to spend time with my boy. Our bond was growing stronger, I was truly appreciating my son, and he *loved* our visits. Every time he saw me coming through the doors, he would race across the room and throw himself into my arms. After *everything* I had done to him—he still loved me, my little Matthew.

But then all of a sudden, Michael, Matthew's father, started saying the visits were upsetting Matthew, then Matthew started missing visits, and soon he stopped showing up altogether. This man (who had never wanted children in the first place) suddenly decided he wanted to keep Matthew, and he didn't want me having contact with him—at all.

So I filed contempt charges, and the visits resumed. But several months later when I went back to court to ask if we could start having unsupervised visits, I was blindsided. Michael told me, "He can't *stand* you! If we can help it, you'll never see him again!" They had a psychiatrist willing to testify that I was an unfit mother and that the visits were damaging to Matthew. I knew this wasn't true, they didn't have a leg to stand on. (Matthew loved our visits; the visit reports were clear on this.) I was poised to say these things, but then Michael said something that stopped me cold.

"If you pursue this, we are going to put Matthew on the stand."

My heart stopped. I could *never* do that to my son. I desperately wanted him back, but there was no *way* I would ever put him through something so cruel; I loved him too much. —He was better off without me.

I cried dry sobs of numbness all the way home. When I arrived I found that my boyfriend had bought some cocaine, so I picked up the pipe and conceded the battle. I was done. I was all done fighting. I was all done caring. I really wanted to be all done living. It was more than I could bear, losing Matthew again.

For days on end, I stayed high. I didn't eat. I didn't sleep. All I wanted to do was press Matthew out of my mind. Then one night I tried to kill myself. I loaded up a needle with crack cocaine, injected it, then loaded it up again. All night long, one after another, I shot into veins that shouldn't even be dreamed of—and I *couldn't* understand *why* I didn't die! "Why won't you let me *DIE!*" I screamed at God. "THERE'S *NOTHING* WORTH LIVING FOR! *NOTHING!* LET ME DIE! *LET—ME—DIE!...*"

I did an entire eight ball of cocaine that night.

A week later I tried to kill myself by walking down the middle of a busy road, and when that didn't work I headed for the bridge, but a police officer picked me up before I reached it.

My boyfriend was getting so fed up with me he threatened to kill me himself. "I'm going to tie you up in the basement and let you starve!"

I calmly begged him, "Would you? Please? End this hell? You can't hurt me any more."

That's when he left me.

At this point I made a desperate phone call to the Psychic Hotline, and I will never forget the tone of the man's voice on the other end. He sounded genuinely surprised when he told me that "the God of the universe" had his hand on my life, and that he loved me very much. He also said that I shouldn't worry—because when my son was thirteen or fourteen years old, he was going to be returned to me.*

Well, since my boyfriend didn't come back, and since I couldn't kill myself, I decided to leave. I thought maybe if I went far enough away, my heart wouldn't hurt so much. So I packed a few things, stepped out onto the sidewalk, and prayed, "Dear God, guide my feet."

I ended up in Florida where I did fairly well for several weeks. I was house-sitting for the trucker who had given me a ride, making good money at a waitressing job, and staying clean and sober. But I was *so* lonely; I missed my boy terribly. At my job, I started buying gumballs and stickers for the kids I waited on, all the while pretending the children were Matthew.

Then my brother passed away. Since he lived only eighty miles from where I was, my family decided I should be the one to take care of his affairs. So I gave notice at my work and went and moved into his house—away from all my new friends. The neighbors across the street were helping me out, and on one of my visits with them I met a relative of theirs. Then one day he showed up at my brother's house asking if I wanted to party. The next thing I knew, we were headed down to crack town.

> **"Stand fast therefore in the liberty wherewith Christ hath made us free, and be not entangled again with the yoke of bondage."**
> (Galatians 5:1)

At the end of July, I was arrested for possession.

I didn't resist. I didn't care. I remember handing the officer the pipe, saying, "You're going to want this." At the jail they left the lights on all night because I couldn't stop crying. I think they thought I was going to try to kill myself.

All night long they watched me until I fell asleep in the early morning hours. When I finally woke up, I saw a group of girls having a Bible study. I was floored! Right there in the jail, these young women had pulled out Bibles and were studying in Collossians, talking about when the apostle Paul was in prison. This really intrigued me.

So when I went back home to my brother's house, I found a little church down the street and started attending services. I also started reading my Bible. I read everything I could about Paul, and as long as I was reading, things were good, but as soon as I put that Bible down, back down the street I went. And I was actually angry at *God*, blaming *him* for my behavior. "Why won't you *stop* me? *I can't stop myself!"* One time lightning struck the road right in front of my jeep—but I kept right on driving.

Trying to come to grips with my shattered heart and fragile mental state was difficult enough without the cocaine. The drug was making me delusional. People at church kept telling me that God loved me and that he would forgive me, but I didn't believe them; I was *so* horrible! I had abused my son. How could God ever forgive that?

But the ladies at church wouldn't give up on me. If I didn't show up on Sunday, inevitably, someone would call or leave a note, telling me that they missed me and that they hoped to see me again. (I had asked for prayer, so they knew I was in trouble.) I would go back to church, I would read my Bible, but I was using every week, and sometimes would drop out of sight for days on end.

Thanksgiving day found me wasted, completely alone, walking down a dark street in a bad part of town. A police officer stopped and gave me a warning. "It isn't safe for you to be out here all alone."

Alone.

I had never been so alone in all my life.

I sold my jeep and bought close to a thousand dollars worth of cocaine. When that was gone, my dealer's cousin came over and did some Christmas shopping in the house. He left me with an empty house and what was supposed to be $200. worth of crack. But when I smoked it, nothing happened, it was completely bogus. So I did the only other thing knew to do. I went into my room, grabbed my Bible, and started reading. When I reached 1Corrinthians 10:13 I stopped and read it again.

"... God is faithful... but will with the temptation also make a way of escape, that ye may be able to bear it. "
(1 Corrinthians 10:13)

Immediately I started praying for this escape. I fell asleep crying, *begging,* for this escape.

The next morning I woke up with an image in my mind. I saw the church, and on the front lawn, my friend Judy Morrill. I hadn't worked since moving to my brother's house, so I often walked down to the church looking for things to do. I would pull weeds, pick up trash, and do whatever else needed to be done. For several weeks I had been doing this, and never once had I seen anyone there. But now I felt that I needed to go there, and that I would find someone.

When I approached the building, I didn't see Judy, but I saw Lem, Judy's husband. I said to him, "Lem, I'm in trouble."

He said, "I know."

"No, Lem," I said. "I'm really in trouble. I need help."

He told me to go sit down in the shade, and that he would call Judy. She came right away and took me to her house.

And we walked.

Her driveway was a mile and a half long. For several days we just walked, back and forth, over and over—and over, until I got through the withdrawals. Then she brought me to her Sunday school class. She had me pass out crayons, help with the kids, help clean up.... and I didn't understand. I remember praying, "Is this a sick joke? I can't see my own child, yet you would allow me to hang around with other people's children? What is this?"

I was still *very* depressed, but I was in a godly place, surrounded by people who loved me, and so gradually, as time went by, I began to care if I survived.

Judy started making phone calls to Christian rehab programs. Most of the places wanted lots of money (which I didn't have) but finally one place said they would take me. They're called *Jesus Is!*. They were in Inglis, Florida, there was no charge, and they had a bed open.

The day Judy drove me down to Inglis was December 19th, 2003, and it is a drive I will never forget. I was trying real hard not to think about anything by focusing on what the preacher on the radio was saying. Since Christmas was just around the corner, he was talking, of course, about the birth of Christ, and about how Jesus came down to earth and became a human so that he could be sacrificed—so that he could save us. Then when the song, *This is my Offering,* came on the radio, I broke. I opened my heart to God, and I prayed, "You gave your only son to save me from my sin. How awesome is that! The least I can do is give my life to you! I can't keep living like this. Besides, you couldn't possibly do any worse than what I've done with my life.

Jesus Is! was unlike anything I had ever experienced. Run completely on donations, it's a bare bones operation. I was put in a dormroom with *sixteen* other women—yet somehow we survived. They kept us working from sun-up to sun-down, and it seemed that whenever an argument broke out, someone would come along, at just the right moment, and start praying. It happend all the time. It was common to walk into a room to find six or eight girls praying and crying.

They kept us up late for Bible studies. "I don't want to hear any complaining!" the director would say. "When you were out there doing drugs, you stayed up *all night* and didn't think a thing of it! Now you're here doing good things in the presence of God, and you're *going* to stay awake! You're *going* to listen to me..."

And miracles happened. We truly believed we had angels protecting us. One hurricane was coming straight toward us, but skirted right around the property. The only thing it touched was the tiny corner of one building that stuck out over the property line! That corner was ripped clean off, but everything else was untouched. The longer I stayed there, the closer I felt to God, and the more I trusted him.

Two months into the program, I decided to write a letter to Michael, Matthew's father. But first I went to some friends and asked them to pray with me. When we finished, one of them said, "Don't worry. God is going to bring Matthew back to you. I don't know how I know this, I just do, but when Matthew is around thirteen, they're going to give him up and turn him over to you." I stared at her in disbelief. It still sounded too good to be true; I still wouldn't allow myself to believe it.

In the letter, I told Michael how much I appreciated him stepping in to take care of Matthew. I thanked both Michael and his wife, Lisa, for the sacrifices they were making and for everything they were doing for Matthew. Then I ended the letter asking them if I might be able to talk with Matthew sometime, *if* they saw fit. I gave them my number and left it at that.

Two weeks later I got a phone call from Matthew's step-mother. She couldn't *believe* I would even *consider* contacting Matthew! I stood frozen, listening as she vented her anger toward me. When she finally stopped, I said calmly, "I'm sorry you feel that way. I understand you're upset with me, you have good reason to be. I just pray that God will bless you."

She hung up.

I think I cried for three days. Then my friend Sheri came to talk with me. She said, "God is going to give you this child back. You just need to trust him. I have one of my own that I don't get to talk to either. I don't know if I'll ever get him back, but somehow I *know* God's going to give Matthew back to you."

Two weeks later, after I had completed my ninety day program and signed on as staff, I received another phone call. It was during a Saturday night sing-along. Now as a rule, no one was allowed to talk on the phone during this time—but someone came in and grabbed me. "You have a phone call!"

It was Lisa again. She wanted to know if I would talk to Matthew.

I said, "Well, YEAH!"

"You have to give me a minute," she said, sounding like she was going to cry. The line was quiet a moment, and then she said, "—He needs a mom. He needs his *real* mom—and I'm not her. He needs to talk to you."

I heard her handing the phone to someone, then I heard his voice.

"Hello."

It was the most beautiful sound I have ever heard in my life.

I asked him, "Are you still My Little Bugaboo?"

He said, "Well, YEAH!"

I stepped outside and for half an hour, as the rain poured down on the tin roof, I talked to my son! This in itself was a miracle because that phone normally *never* stopped ringing, but for that precious half-hour the call-waiting never beeped in once. Before I hung up, I thanked Lisa and told her, if she saw fit, I would love to talk to him again sometime. I left it up to her to set the perameters. I then went back in to the sing-along and had the most beautiful night ever!

A few months passed, and I sent Matthew a birthday card. Then Lisa called back. This time she was mean again! "I can't believe you think you should have any part in this child's life! Don't call! Don't bother us! *And don't send him anything!*"

I was *devastated!* I had no idea what I had done wrong—but I did understand her desire to protect Matthew. So I went out on the porch and started praying, and the Lord spoke to my heart. I felt him telling me that Matthew *would* be given back, and that together we would do God's will. As I sat there wondering *how* this could possibly happen, I felt the Lord say, "Don't worry if it's possible. I'll take care of that."

I finished my year as a staff trainee then started planning to go visit my mother in Maine for two weeks. Before I left, I mustered up the courage to call Michael. I told him that I would really like to spend a little time with Matthew *if* it was alright with them.

Six hours! They gave me *six* hours! I hadn't seen him in *three years,* so I could hardly contain myself! My mother and I took him to church (Matthew had always loved Calvary Chapel), we took him out to dinner, then I gave him the choice of going to a park or to Leonard's Mills. He chose Leonard's Mills, and we had a *blast!* It didn't matter that we were both a little nervous, and it didn't matter that it was *freezing* cold and I was wearing clogs and a light jacket. Matthew and I went to this outdoor museum in the Maine woods and had so much fun together, exploring, throwing rocks in the stream, playing… Matthew was talking and laughing and having a wonderful time.

But as soon as we went back to his father's house, he changed right before my eyes. He sort of went inside himself, all of the fun and laughter we had been sharing was suddenly gone.

Back in Florida, several months later, I sent Matthew another birthday present. And once again I got a phone call telling me to *stay out of his life!*

How was he ever going to be a part of my life if they kept going back and forth between, *"We can't stand you!"* to *"He needs you, will you please talk to him?"*

Another year went by with no contact, and Matthew turned twelve. I had only seen him once in three years and only talked to him twice. Waiting was *torture*. But I kept praying. And waiting. And praying some more.

Then I began to suspect there was something wrong with my mother. She wasn't answering her phone, which was very unlike her, and when she did answer she sounded terrible. So I headed back to Maine to take care of her.

After a few weeks I called Matthew's grandparents on his father's side to let them know I was in the area and to ask them how Matthew was doing. I didn't want to upset anyone, I just thought they might give me some information. Grammy told me what she knew, and I didn't push for anything else.

Two days later Lisa called. She wanted to know if I wanted to see Matthew again.

Sunday morning we went to church together. Then I brought him straight home. We walked up to the porch, and I stepped inside with him. I told them where we had gone, and that we had had a good time. I was trying very hard not to offend anyone, doing what I thought a good parent would do. But the next day I got a phone call. Michael told me to *never* set foot inside *her* house again!

A week later I got another phone call. It was Michael. "You need to come over. We need to talk right *now.*"

So I was thinking, *What* have I done *now?* I was scared to death! I called the church, I called *Jesus Is!,* and I called Judy. I asked everyone to please *pray* because I had no idea what I was walking into, and I couldn't bear the thought of losing Matthew again. So everyone started praying, and I drove to Matthew's house.

They invited me in. They asked me to sit down. Then they proceeded to tell me how Matthew had been increasingly getting into trouble. He'd been caught shoplifting and was brought home by the police, and they were at their wits end. They couldn't deal with him anymore. Then Michael said the most beautiful thing I had ever heard. *"Would you be willing to take him home with you?"*

My jaw hit the floor. "Well, *YEAH!*"

Matthew ran into his room, grabbed the bag he had already packed, and together we walked out the door.

He was thirteen years old.
And he's been with me ever since.

Two months after going back with his mother, Matthew stood up in church and accepted Jesus Christ as his Lord and Savior. One week after that he was baptised. Matthew is now sixteen years old and attends Calvary Chapel Christian School where he (almost) never gets into trouble.

On May 20th, 2009, Barbara and Michael went back to court, only this time in total agreement. They appealed to the court to ammend the original judgement to provide for shared custody, with Barbara being the primary residence. The judge granted this request. He also cancelled Barbara's $7,500. debt of back child support by cancelling it out against Michael's future debt.

And Barbara says, "We serve a mighty, awesome, amazingly majestic God who is able to do above and beyond all that we could ever imagine!"

*I don't recommend EVER calling one of these hotlines! That one call cost over $400.00! After the "psychic" gave me the message about my son, he kept me on the line for close to twenty minutes, telling me all kinds of other things that never came to pass. However, this experience did show me that God can use *anyone* to accomplish his purposes!

To learn more about Jesus Is!
go to www.jesusis.com

Heaven Bound
Belinda's Story

I always thought my son was going to be a missionary. And in a way he is, only, not in the way I thought he would be.

> Benjamin Joel Townsend, 19, died June 11, 2002. He was born Sept. 30, 1982, in Bangor, the son of Dennis and Belinda Townsend. Ben enjoyed fishing, skateboarding, and he loved animals.... Ben was loved by all who knew him and will be greatly missed...

My son Benjamin was quite the character, so full of life, love, and hope that he could rarely contain himself. He would often hug or kiss me or his dad, even in public, even when he became a teenager. In fact he never hesitated to express his affection for anyone. And not only was he fun-loving and outgoing, but he was always very considerate. Whenever he came in after being out late, he always made sure that we knew he was home safe. He would stop by our bedroom door and say in a loud whisper, "Mom—Mom—I'm home. I'm okay."

He was a blessing in many ways.

When Ben was only four years old, he asked Jesus into his heart, then immediately started telling anyone who would listen all about it. He understood that his sins had been forgiven so that he could go to heaven, and he wanted everyone else to know this too. In fact, he shared with so many people, we started calling him "Our Little Preacher." Throughout his childhood and early teen years he was never afraid to tell others what he was learning about God, and because of this, I thought for sure he would someday be a missionary.

When he got a little older, he started getting into extreme sports, like karate, skateboarding, snowboarding, mountain biking… You name it. If it was dangerous, he wanted to do it.

Maybe that's why he got caught up in the drug scene.

At seventeen, we started noticing a difference in him. At first it was subtle, but after awhile we knew something was definitely wrong. By the time he was willing to come clean about what he was doing, he was fully addicted. It was the hardest decision we ever had to make, but we told him he would not be allowed to live at home if he continued on the path he was on.

Ultimately he ended up at U-Turn 4 Christ, a Christian discipleship/rehab program, where he was able to get off drugs, and where he recommitted his life to the Lord.

After the program he found a place of his own and continued to do well. He got a job with a landscaping business, and was paying his bills. He was staying clean and sober, and taking care of himself. *And* he was accepted into the Marines. He was on a delayed entry and still had a couple of classes to take in order to earn his GED, but he was already a sworn in Marine. And we were very proud of him. The Benjamin we knew and loved was back, and things were really looking up for him. That is, until he got injured on the job.

All day they had been digging up small trees and wrapping them in burlap to be transported to another location. It was raining so, as the day wore on, the burlap and the soil got heavier and heavier. Ben was not a muscular guy, and as he was trying to lift one of these rain soaked bundles, his back went out. The pain was excruciating, but the bosses accused him of faking! They insisted that he was lying to get out of doing the hard work, and that they were going to prove it. But he wasn't faking, he really couldn't work. He tried going back to work several times, but always ended up needing to go home.

The doctor told him he would soon heal, and sent him to a chiropractor, but after a month the pain was getting worse. He couldn't work, and he was having more and more trouble just taking care of himself. So we packed up his few belongings and brought him home.

We realized right away that he wasn't sleeping; his light was on all night, every night. And not only was he in constant pain, but he was also having muscle spasms in his legs. Then he confided in me that he was losing his bowels. He visited the doctor again, but still nothing was done. Then one Sunday night on the way to church, my nineteen year old son started crying. *"Mom, I can't take this pain anymore! I can't do it! I JUST can't!"*

I told him, "We'll get you into the doctor's again tomorrow. We will find out what's going on."

On Monday, they said they couldn't take him until Tuesday. Tuesday when he came down the stairs he looked like he hadn't slept in a month. "Mom, I can't drive. I… I…. can't function. I can't do anything. Can Dad drive me?"

I hugged him and told him yes. I told him not to worry, and that everything was going to be okay. And I told him I loved him.

At the doctor's they said he would have to have a CT scan—but they wouldn't be able to fit him in for another *week*.

It was our 25th wedding anniversary, and my husband, Dennis, had brought twenty-five red roses into my work. I love roses, and we had a nice visit, but about a half an hour after he left, the phone rang. It was Dennis. He was frantic! Ben was gone—and he had left a note.

> *Mom. Dad. I can't take this*
> *pain anymore. I can't do it.*
> *I'll see you in heaven.*

When I got home, Dennis was on the phone with the sheriff, and the note was on the breakfast bar. I read it, and somehow I *knew* where he had gone. There was no doubt in my mind. I told Dennis I was going down to Ben's fishing spot. He said he had already gone down there. He said he had seen his car, but Ben was nowhere to be found.

I headed for the door.

"The sheriff said not to go looking for him!"

I jumped into my car. There was no *way* they were going to stop me from looking for my son!

"I'm telling you, he's not there. *I already looked!*"

First I saw his car, then I saw him—right where I knew he would be. I yelled, but he didn't move, so I moved closer. He was wearing his bright yellow skateboarding shirt. He was slumped over. I didn't touch him, I just looked at him, and I knew he was gone. He had shot himself.

Back at the house, people started showing up.
A flurry of activity.
Pastor Ken and Jeanette showed up.
People kept coming.
People—everywhere.
My head—buzzing.
My heart—struggling.
In a fog.
Choking.
I can't…
I can't…

I went into the living room and looked up at Pastor Ken. "Can we… Could you…" I took a breath. "Can you read to me—from scripture? That's all I want right now."

So Ken, Jeanette, and I found a quiet place, and it was good. Just hearing scripture. So I could calm myself down.

When we came back out my son Dennis (Denny), who is a police officer, had arrived. He was very concerned for me because of what I had seen. But as I talked to him, I realized I hadn't seen anything—or maybe I just couldn't remember… I must have seen every detail, because I knew Ben had shot himself, but I couldn't remember! I could picture his yellow tee-shirt and his jeans—but that was all.

Belinda believes God protected her by not allowing her to see the graphic details of her son's death. She also believes God protected her husband. The gun used was Dennis' new shotgun. If Dennis had seen it, he most likely would have picked it up and left fresh fingerprints, which would have made him a suspect in his son's death.

People kept coming, so I went up to my room and stood by my bed. "How am I going to do this?" I pleaded with God. "Please help me through this. I don't… I can't… Please God…" And then my mind started racing. Is this MY fault? Why didn't Dennis…? Why didn't WE do something? Why didn't the doctor DO something?!

In my panic I felt the Lord speak. I didn't hear words, but I knew in my heart what he was saying. "Belinda. Satan meant this for evil, but you have a choice to make. If you will do my will, this will turn into a blessing beyond your wildest dreams. I will comfort you. I will take care of you. I will do whatever it takes to get you through this."

I stood frozen, with tears streaming down my face—and I made my choice. I would not be bitter, I would not be angry, I was not going to blame anyone.

"Do not let evil defeat you; instead, conquer evil with good."
(Romans 12:21)

Immediately I knew what God wanted from me. I was to share what had happened to Ben because it would minister to others. I would not hide the fact that he had committed suicide. I said in my heart, *Lord, if this is what you want, I will do it.* Then something unexplainable happened. It was as though the warmest, softest blanket wrapped itself around me, and strong arms held me tight. "I will hold you together. I will get you through this." I felt the Lord say.

And there was peace.

The very next day I woke up, but had not yet opened my eyes, when I heard a loud whisper. *"Mom.*

Mom. I'm okay." It was Ben's voice. I looked around. At first I thought I was losing my mind. But once again I knew. It wasn't really Ben speaking to me, I was sure of this, but the Lord wanted me to hear his voice, so I would know he was safe in heaven. I already knew this, but hearing his voice cemented it for me.

And again I had peace.

I didn't want to get up. I wanted to stay there forever, resting in the assurance that Ben was okay—and that I would be okay too.

When we walked into the funeral parlor, my head was spinning. When they started showing us caskets, I almost passed out. I looked at my husband, and he read my thoughts. *I can't do this! I can't! And we don't have this kind of money!* Pastor Ken saw our panic and stepped in. First he asked for the cheapest casket, then he asked if he could take it to the church. We had no idea what he was going to do.

When we walked into the funeral service, I was in awe. Ben's brother, Brandon, had brought in a collection of Ben's things and had made a sort of celebration of his life around the room. There were his Karate gi, his fishing poles, his skateboard, candles (Ben loved candles)… all of the things that were Ben. A wonderful collage of photos was set up by the casket. And the casket! Ben had always wanted to get a tattoo like Pastor Ken's, so Ken had painted a sword on the top and had also drawn a picture of Jesus on the cross. It was absolutely amazing! I had no idea Ken was such a talented artist. And not only this, but the casket was covered with scriptures. Everyone who attended that funeral that day (and there were *many*) all had the opportunity to read God's promises and to see God's amazing love at work. It was absolutely unbelievable what these people did for us.

Among all of Ben's things that were on display at the funeral, one thing stands out most clearly in my memory. A simple notebook. On the front where it had once said "Spiral Bound" Ben had scratched off the word "Spiral" and replaced it with the word "Heaven." HEAVEN BOUND.

This was not just a service to let people say goodbye to a young man, it contained a message of hope. Ben had given his life to the Lord at a very young age. The Bible tells us, to be saved you must trust in Jesus' redeeming work on the cross. Ben had always believed this. Even though he had fallen into sin and ultimately taken his own life, God's promise still stood.

***"Because if you confess
the Lord Jesus with your mouth,
and believe in your heart that God raised Him
from the dead, you will be saved."***
(Romans 10:9 LITV)

It was a beautiful, beautiful June day for the committal service. There wasn't a cloud in the sky—but at the end while everyone was still standing with heads bowed, I looked up—and there it was. Right near the sun, a perfect rainbow.

I stood transfixed.

"This is amazing," I heard Pastor Ken say.

Then Denny said, "Mom, turn around."

I turned, and my mouth dropped open. On the other side of the sky, there was another rainbow, only this one was upside down!

> *A colorful smile in the sky. The viewing of an upside down rainbow, or what is properly called a "circumzenithal arc," is a very rare occurrence. They are brighter and more colorful than normal rainbows and usually occur in cold regions. These brilliant upside down arcs are formed in a clear sky when sunlight bounces off non-terminated, horizontally-oriented ice crystals high in the atmosphere. The arcs themselves are not uncommon, but, since they are usually obscured by low level clouds, viewing one of them from the ground is extremely rare.*

In the weeks after Ben's death people kept telling us that we should sue the doctors. When we described Ben's symptoms to a friend of the family, who is a physician's assistant, she was certain that Ben had been suffering with a herniated disc. He should have been put on strong pain medication and may have needed surgery. But because of the increase in pain medication abuse (teenagers were faking symptoms to get pain pills) kids with legitimate issues were being under-treated. She was sure this is what had happened with Ben. She was sure we would win the case if we sued. But she knew we wouldn't.

Every one of the people who under-treated Ben will forever have to live with the fact that Ben took his life because of their negligence. That is punishment enough. If we had sued, what good would that have done? How horrible would our lives be if we had chosen to blame and take revenge? I can only imagine the bitterness, the hostility, and the anger that would have resulted.

> ***"Do not pay others back evil for evil… Instead, bless them, because you were called to inherit a blessing… turn away from evil and do good… seek peace and pursue it."***
> (1 Peter 3:9; 3:11 ISV)

The chiropractor who was treating Ben saw in the paper that Ben had died, and he called us. Though many thought we should have sued this man, we instead chose to share the Gospel with him.

> ***"…Be ready at all times to answer anyone who asks you to explain the hope you have in you,"***
> (I Peter 3:15 GNB)

When things died down we began to hear how Ben's funeral had affected people. People started calling and sending letters, or pulling me aside at work. At the funeral the Gospel had been clearly presented by one of the pastors. As a result three people were saved that day. One of those people was my boss' husband. The others were kids who had learned about the Lord from Ben.

It's been eight years since my son went to be with the Lord, but the opportunities to share his story continue to this day. Usually at least a few times a month my husband

and I are able to minister to others who are going through hard times. And when someone in crisis hears Ben's story they listen differently. They want to know how we ever got through it. We tell them the Lord got us through. We chose to cling to him and to his word, and *he* got us through. In a world where suicide often results in the devastation of a family, we are able to show how following God not only held us together, but ultimately made us stronger on the other side.

My husband works with teenagers. Every once in awhile one of them will try (or threaten) to kill himself. When Dennis goes to talk to them they will often reject him saying things like, "What do you know? You have a good life! You've never been through anything bad!..." This opens the door for him to lovingly tell them about Ben, and to help them through their crisis.

> ***"...God turned it into good,
> in order to preserve the lives of many people
> who are alive today because of what happened."***
> (Genesis 50:20 GNB)

It's absolutely amazing what this child gave us. He gave us hope. He gave us love, a lot of love. But in the tragedy he gave us more. How many parents have the opportunity to share God's love and the hope of eternal life through their son's death? I miss him every day, and it doesn't get any easier telling Ben's story, but it does get more blessed. I don't believe it was God's plan for Ben to take his life. But it happened, and it's helping people come to know the Lord, so that makes it okay.

I believe it points us right back to the cross—how God gave *his* son for us.

"For God so loved the world,
that he gave his only begotten Son,
that whosoever believeth in him should not
perish, but have everlasting life."
(John 3:16 KJV)

He scratched off the word "Spiral"
and replaced it with the word,
"Heaven."

Ben knew where he was going.

The Gift
Joan's Story

As I strolled through the aisles of the small town grocery store, I gathered several items into my cart, then headed for the checkout.

The cashier quietly totaled up and bagged my order, and I paid her. But before I could step away, she piped up. "Are you sure you aren't forgetting anything?"

Thinking this was weird, I gave her a look. "Ah—I don't think so."

With this she flashed a brilliant smile, reached beneath the small counter, then pulled up a large fully decorated Christmas tree. It was the most perfect tree I had ever seen. "Here," she said, "this is for you."

I stood with my mouth open. "Are you sure?"

"Yes. Take it. It's free."

"Thank you!" I said, carefully balancing the tree in my cart. I wanted to ask her where it came from, why it was free, and if everyone was getting one, but someone stepped in behind me. Not wanting to hold up traffic, I began to push my cart forward.

"Are you sure you aren't forgetting anything?" It was the cashier again.

This time I smiled in anticipation and repeated, "I don't think so."

Again she reached beneath the counter. This time she brought up the biggest, most beautiful Easter basket I had ever seen. Brightly wrapped candies and decorated chocolates almost spilled over the edge. Sparkling ribbons and trinkets decorated the outside. My eyes were wide, and her eyes sparkled as she handed it over. I could hardly believe my good fortune.

Quickly I began to push the cart homeward; somehow I knew I needed to get home before I could dig into my treasures. I rushed along thinking to myself, *I need to get home, get home, get home...*

But before I could get home, I woke up—and was, once again, a tiny girl snuggled beneath the covers of my bed. Excitement melted into disappointment as I reached down and plucked Teddy from the floor. I hugged him tight and squeezed my eyes shut—but sleep would not come. My treasures were gone. Oh *why* hadn't I eaten the candies? *Why* did I have to get home first?

I was not quite four years old when I had this dream, yet I remember it still today, some thirty-five years later. I was an adult in the dream, and it was very real. How could I, a tiny child, know what it felt like to be an adult? I always thought this was the reason why I never forgot the dream, but perhaps there was a greater purpose.

Many years passed, and I don't remember exactly when I first began listening to the Christian radio network, CSN International, but once I started I was *hooked*. I'd always wanted to read the Bible, but I had never made it past Genesis on my own. CSN was a gold mine! What a blessing! I learned so much from the pastors on the radio: the meaning of repentance, evidence for creation, the inerrancy of scripture, why there is evil in the world... and that Calvary Chapel pastors are all just a little bit nutty. But this is okay because God uses the foolish things of the world to confound the wise. Right? (I learned that from CSN too.) But seriously, I was hearing the word, my faith was growing, and I recommitted my life to Jesus.

Then one night as I sat listening to a teaching about the fact that salvation cannot be earned, it hit me! That dream I'd had all those years ago contained a message! It was all about the gift. *The* gift. Jesus.

I *paid* for the groceries, but the tree and the basket were *free*. I hadn't done anything to earn them. All I needed to do was accept them. A Christmas tree and an Easter basket, symbols of Jesus' arrival on earth and of his resurrection from the dead!

To be saved all we need to do is accept the *free gift*—which God holds out with a smile.

> **"For by grace are ye saved through faith; and that not of yourselves: it is the gift of God: Not of works, lest any man should boast."**
> (Ephesians 2:8-9 KJV)

When I was a tiny child, God had planted the message of the Gospel in my heart. Subsequently it wasn't until I became an adult (as I was in the dream) that I accepted Jesus as my Savior, and the hole in my heart was filled to overflowing with his Spirit (like the candies in the basket).

And another thing I believe the dream revealed: Those of us who have accepted the free gift of salvation will not truly taste the gifts God has given us until we leave this world and join him in eternity.

And wouldn't it be just like our precious Savior to have that beautiful Easter basket waiting for me when I *finally* do make it home?

Taylor
Betsy's Story

He told us we needed to abort this "fetus" right away.
But we said no.

I was eleven weeks pregnant with my first baby when I went to my first appointment. I went alone because I never thought anything would be wrong. But when they did the ultrasound, there it was. It stretched from the top of her head all the way down to her shoulder blades—and it was full of fluid. They sent me straight to the hospital for a more detailed ultrasound, then it was back to my doctor's office, where I sat waiting—for a half an hour. When the nurse finally brought me in to speak to the doctor, he gently told me that it looked to him, like Turner's syndrome.

> *Turner's syndrome is a chromosomal disorder that affects approximately one in every 2,500 females where a mutation occurs in which all or part of one of the X chromosomes is absent. Only 2% of babies diagnosed with Turner's syndrome survive until birth.*

He thought it was Turner's, but he couldn't be sure until I was checked by a specialist—and strangely enough, I had peace.

Two weeks later my husband Jim went with me to see the specialist. The doctor explained, in order to make an accurate diagnosis, he would have to do an amniocentisis. A needle would be inserted into my abdomen to remove a sample of amniotic fluid for testing.

An ultrasound was performed during the procedure, so we could see the baby, and what we saw was amazing! When the needle entered the sack, the baby backed away as far as she could get. Then she started swatting at it with her arms, like she was trying to get away from it. Jim and I looked at each other in awe. There was no doubt about what we were looking at. Here was not just a thing, or a lump of tissue, or whatever else they try to make you think it is. It was a baby, *our* baby, and she knew what was going on!

Two weeks later we went back to get the results. This time we first met with a geneticist. She explained to us that Turner's syndrome is not a hereditary thing, but a mutation. It was not caused by something a couple did, or had, or anything like that, but sometimes, for no reason whatsoever, it just happened.

When the doctor came in he told us it was definitely Turner's. He explained that if it was *only* Turner's, there would be a chance she might survive—but it wasn't only Turner's. She also had the sack of fluid called a cystic hygroma. According to all the textbooks, no child with Turner's syndrome *and* a cystic hygroma had *ever* survived. He told us we needed to abort this "fetus" right away. It was going to die, and when that happened, there was a high likelihood I would get toxemia, which would put *my* life at risk.

But we said no. He looked at us with a "Come again?" expression. So we repeated, no, we would not abort this baby. Ever.

Everything in his demeanor told us he couldn't believe we were that stupid. I don't remember if he actually used the word stupid, but he told us in no uncertain terms that we were foolish, or idiots to do this. He said, "There's no way this child is going to live!" But we would not change our minds. So he walked out.

We were quite shaken up, and even the geneticist had tears in her eyes. She looked like she wanted to punch him! So we left there, not on very good terms, but we knew we had made the right decision. We had no right to take the life of our baby. Neither did he.

So I went back to my gynecologist. He said, "Well, I will take the best care of you that I can, and if you do decide to abort this baby, I can do that—if you change your mind." We told him we were not going to change our minds. –Somehow I knew God was taking care of us.

During this time, Jim and I were doing a lot of praying, but I was uncertain. What should I pray? Do I pray for her to live? What if we don't know how to take care of her? Do I pray for myself? I struggled with selfish feelings. This is what I want: I want her to live and be healthy. *But what if that wasn't God's plan?* Eventually I came to the place where it was settled in my heart. When I finally said, "God, *Your* will be done, it's in Your hands," there was peace again.

So knowing that she could die at any moment, I continued to go in for appointments—and things went from bad to worse. They found more fluid pockets. I don't remember how many, but there were at least two in her brain and one in her heart. Wow. This was NOT good! They told us these pockets, called nonimmune hydrops, could cause major problems, but there was nothing they could do about them, until she was born.

If she made it that far.

I don't know how many prayer chains we were on, but, as far as I know, we had people from Maine to California praying that God would heal this child. Both Jim and I were part of Campus Crusades, so they were praying. My aunt in Houlton had a bunch of people praying, and we had one friend who prayed for her every day.

> *"... Jesus... said unto them,*
> *With men this is impossible; but with God*
> *all things are possible."*
> (Matthew 19:26 KJV)

When I first started feeling her kick, I was at first amazed and then worried. If she was moving I knew she was okay, but if she was quiet for awhile, well, how long was normal? How long should I wait before becoming concerned? *Is she just sleeping, or is she...* Then she would kick again! And she just kept on kicking! So people continued to pray.

When I was seven and a half months pregnant the specialist was back in town, so my doctor scheduled another appointment. When Jim and I walked into the examining room, the specialist didn't say much. When he did the ultrasound, he didn't saying anything at all.

So I asked, "—Well? Is she okay?"

He remained quiet. When finally he spoke, he said, "She should be dead by now." When we asked him why she had survived, he said, "—I don't know. I don't understand this. She should be dead. No child has ever lived with this."

Almost all of the fluid pockets had disappeared.

He shook his head. "I guess she just didn't read the textbook." He kept on saying this. "She didn't read the textbook."

But we knew *he* didn't read the *right* book. The Bible tells us that the Lord is our healer and that nothing is impossible with God!

Finally he said, "Well, she's gone this long. She's strong. The sack on her neck is still there, but I guess she'll probably make it to term."

The first thing my mom did was go out and buy a baby outfit, little pink overalls. Up to this point no one had dared to do anything, but now baby showers were scheduled, and everybody started buying stuff, pink stuff.

Then, on August 17th, 1994, Taylor was born.

A cesarean section was done because of complications the fluid sack presented. But she could have been delivered naturally because the sack—was gone. She scored a nine on the Apgar test (ten is the highest), and when the nurse looked her over, she said, "She's fine. Look. Her arms, her legs, her hands, everything, they work!"

> *"I will praise thee;*
> *for I am fearfully and wonderfully*
> *made…"*
> (Psalm 139:14 KJV)

Today Taylor is a fifteen-year-old normal little kid. She does have Turner's syndrome with some of the typical physical attributes, but she is not disabled in any way. She plays soccer, she rides horseback, and she is home schooled along with her three younger siblings. She sometimes struggles with certain math or science concepts (because of the missing X chromosome she should have gotten from her father) but she works hard to overcome this and has always been a self-motivated, responsible, hard working young lady. Taylor has made a personal decision for Christ and wants to live her life affecting others for him. She has recently been talking about working with abused children or animals.

Other than some minor heart problems she's had since birth, Taylor is perfectly healthy.

He told us we needed to abort this "fetus" right away. But we said no.

"Blessed is the man that walketh not in the counsel of the ungodly..."
(Psalm 1:1 KJV)

The following scripture
is taken from the Gospel of John,
but it is also true for
Miracles.

***"... Jesus performed
many other miracles which are not
written down in this book.***

***But these have been
written in order that you may believe
that Jesus is the Messiah, the Son of God,
and that through your faith in him
you may have life."***
(John 20:30-31 GNB)

It's simple. Have faith in Jesus, who died on the cross for your sins, that you might have life.

—Everlasting life. It's a free gift! All you need to do is reach out and accept it. If you have never had your sins forgiven, and do not know that you will go to heaven when you die, you can pray a prayer something like this:

Dear Father in heaven,

I need forgiveness. I believe that Jesus came and died on the cross so my sins could be forgiven. Please forgive me. And, Lord Jesus, please come into my heart and change me. Help me live for you.

Amen.

If you do not know the Lord well enough to trust him with your eternal spirit, get to know him, read the Bible.

(Don't know where to start? Try the Gospel of John, or the book of Romans.)

Want to learn about more miracles?
Read the Bible.

The Romans Road

Some think they will go to heaven because they have lived a good life, but the Bible says:

"For all have sinned and fall short of the glory of God."
(Romans 3:23)

"As it is written, There is none righteous, no not one..."
(Romans 3:10)

Sin results in spiritual death, eternal separation from God where there will be "weeping and gnashing of teeth." (Matthew 25:30) But Jesus died to reconnect us spiritually to God, and to save us from hell.

"For the wages of sin is death; but the gift of God is eternal life through Jesus Christ our Lord."
(Romans 6:23)

The Lord suffered and died to make this gift possible because he loves us.

"God demonstrates his own love for us, in that while we were yet sinners Christ died for us!"
(Romans 5:8)

If you feel the Lord knocking on your heart, open the door and let him in. Ask him to forgive you and save you.

"If you confess with your mouth Jesus as Lord, and believe in your heart that God raised Jesus from the dead, you shall be saved;"
(Romans 10:9)

Don't you hate it when you forget to put the trash out on collection day, so that you end up running out of garbage cans and are forced to store bags full of fermenting garbage in your kitchen, or on the back porch, or wherever? It doesn't take long before the whole place really starts to *stink*.

Well, what if there was a neighborhood where you could put your garbage out anytime (day or night) and the trash man would come instantly and whisk it away?

Spiritually speaking, there is such a neighborhood.

But—what if in that neighborhood there were some who wouldn't admit that they had any garbage at all? What if instead of putting their trash out, they hid it in the rafters, and in the basement, and under their bed... ? Maybe they might even think, *If the trash man wants my garbage, he can come in and get it!* But garbage collectors don't break into people's houses and steal their trash. Neither will the One who takes away sin do it without your permission.

GOD WILL TAKE AWAY YOUR SIN, day or night, but He won't do it unless you put it out there. All you have to do is say in your heart, "God I have sinned. I believe Jesus died so that my sins might be removed. Please take away my sin. Make me clean."

Don't sit around wondering why your life stinks. Put your trash out there. The Lord will take it. Day or night.

> *"And ye know that he (Jesus) was manifested to take away our sins;..."*
> (1John 3:5 KJV)

> *"As far as the east is from the west, (So) far has He removed our transgressions from us."*
> (Psalm 103:12 NKJV)

If you liked ***Miracles***
then perhaps you'll enjoy these novels
edited by Joanie Hileman:

Messages
by John Michael Hileman

Vrin: ten mortal gods
by John Michael Hileman